INTEGRAL VIPASSANA

Mindfulness through Psychology, Neuroscience,
and the Satipatthāna Sutta

Fernando Rodríguez Bornaetxea
and Andrew A.H. Molloy

www.highpointpubs.com

Copyright © 2023 by Fernando Rodríguez Bornaetxea
and Andrew A.H. Molloy

All rights reserved. Published in the United States of America. No part of this book may be reproduced or transmitted in any form or by any means, graphic, electronic, or mechanical, including photocopying, recording, taping, or by any information storage or retrieval system, without permission in writing from the publisher.

This edition published by Highpoint Life Books
For information, write to info@highpointpubs.com.

First Edition

ISBN: 979-8-9879203-5-0

Library of Congress Cataloging-in-Publication Data

Rodriguez and Molloy
Integral Vipassana:
Mindfulness through Psychology, Neuroscience, and the Satipatthāna Sutta

Summary: "This book peals back the layers of one of the most effective movements in Buddhist meditation, relating Buddha's teachings to contemporary neuropsychology and the integral mindset!"
–Provided by publisher.

ISBN: 979-8-9879203-5-0 (Paperback)
1. Meditation 2. Buddhism

Library of Congress Control Number: 2023915348

Cover and Interior Design by Sarah M. Clarehart

Manufactured in the United States of America

ENDORSEMENTS

"Integral Vipassana is a very good, very important book. It not only gives the basics of Integral Vipassana itself, it sets them out in an Integral framework, thus illuminating some of the limitations of meditation in general, while filling it in with other, more integrative material. This makes it a very significant publication, and one I would certainly recommend."
—**Ken Wilber**, bestselling author of *A Brief History of Everything* and *The Integral Vision*

"An insightful commentary on Satipatthana and the concept of sati in contemporary cognitive psychological terms. Fernando Rodriguez Bornaetxea skillfully dismantles the concept of mindfulness in the context of mnemonic processes—providing the reader with a fresh perspective on a fundamental concept for meditation."
—**David R. Vago, Ph.D.**, Director of the Contemplative Neurosciences and Mind-Body Research Laboratory, Vanderbilt University

"An important and valuable book, and one that does the tough job of synthesizing modern science and ancient wisdom in ways that make each feel more complete than they were before. There is great insight here, and I learned a lot reading it."
—**Taylor Plimpton**, author and contributor to *Tricycle: The Buddhist Review*

"In Integral Vipassana, the authors offer an unflinchingly candid exploration of the origins of existential dissatisfaction and the intricacies of the 'I'. With kindness, and without oversimplification, they adeptly synthesize the practice of vipassana, first person subjective experience and modern neuroscience, crafting an invaluable guide for each reader's unique journey towards freedom from suffering."
—Dr. Andrea Grabovac, clinical psychiatrist, author and Co-Director of North American chapter of Mindfulness-integrated Cognitive Behavioral Therapy (MiCBT) Institute

"For anyone invested in the exploration of consciousness, meditation, and psychology, this book stands as a pivotal read. It offers a rich, interdisciplinary approach, connecting profound, ancient wisdom with modern psychological insights, creating a comprehensive guide to understanding the human mind and spirit. In a world brimming with transient pleasures and constant turmoil, Rodriguez and Molloy have given us a sanctuary of wisdom and tranquility. It offers a transformative journey through the landscapes of the mind, granting readers the tools and knowledge to cultivate a life of mindfulness and inner peace. Whether you are a spiritual aspirant, a student of psychology, or simply someone seeking to understand the deeper realms of existence, this interdisciplinary text serves as a beacon, guiding you through the profound realms of Vipassana meditation and beyond."
—Robb Smith, CEO and co-founder, Integral Life

"I am so happy that Fernando has produced a new book in English with Andrew's invaluable collaboration, so that many more readers can be reached. Fernando has been studying and practicing Vipassana with me for about thirty years, and for many years now he has been teaching this remarkable meditation, the development of wisdom and mindfulness. This present book of his deals with Satipatthāna in all its details so that the reader can gain clearer knowledge of the subject, which can then be translated into more effective practice. The enormous knowledge and broad experience that the author possesses will certainly help throw a bright light on the subject for readers. It is essential to have a sound knowledge of Vipassana so that practice may be effective. Only with effective practice can full realization be

achieved, the immeasurable liberation gained through wisdom, or paññāvimutti in Pali, the language of the Buddha. I wish Integral Vipassana tremendous success."
—Dhiravamsa Vipassanācarya

"*Finally, a truly contemporary commentary on the Satipatthāna Sutta that goes beyond sectarian discussions. Fernando Rodríguez Bornaetxea unfolds all his experience as a meditation teacher to dismantle myths and superfluous baggage that we unnecessarily project on meditative practice. What emerges is a fresh path that maintains the original spirit of the Buddha's message: the cultivation of mindfulness. In short, a text of extraordinary lucidity; an inseparable companion in our practice.*"
—Agustin Pániker, Lecturer in The History of Religions, writer, and director of Kairós Publishing

"*These two things play a part in realization. What two? Serenity and discernment.*

What is the benefit of developing serenity? The mind is developed. What is the benefit of developing the mind? Greed is given up. What is the benefit of developing discernment? Wisdom is developed. What is the benefit of developing wisdom? Ignorance is given up. The mind contaminated by greed is not free, and wisdom contaminated by ignorance does not grow. In this way, freedom of heart comes from the fading away of greed, while freedom by wisdom comes from the fading away of ignorance."

—Anguttara Nikaya, 2:31

I managed to finish this book thanks to my companion, Mayu, and her affection, happiness, and loyalty, and also to my master, Dhiravamsa, who showed me the path.

—Fernando

Dedicated to my long-suffering wife, Arrate, with immense gratitude for everything she has given me, particularly my interest in psychology and Buddhism.

—Andrew

CONTENTS

Foreword xv
Preface xix
   Vipassana xx
   The "I" xxii
   The Integral Perspective xxiii
   Other Influences xxvi
      Basic Psychology xxvi
      Affective Neuroscience and Neuropsychoanalysis xxvii
      Neurophenomenology xxvii
      Cognitive Neuroscience xxviii
      Dhamma xxviii
      Ethics xxviii
      Insight xxviii
   A Companion on the Road xxix

Part One
BUDDHISM, VIPASSANA, AND OUR WORLD

Introduction 3
   Buddha and His Time 3
   An Era of Transformation 4
   Scripture and Pali 5
   The Councils and the Pali Canon 7
   Enter Vipassana Meditation 11
      Vipassana Gains Traction 14

Integral Vipassana

    The States of Absorption 16
    The Satipatthāna Sutta 19
        Three Complete Versions, and More 21
        A Guide for Insightful Meditation 22
    How To Read This Book 24
        Chapter Structure: Three Texts 26

1 The Development of Conscious Awareness 29
    The Four Foundations of Attention 30
        Satipatthāna Sutta: The Four Foundations of Mindfulness 31
    Intention 32
    Attention 33
    Approach: The First Three Paragraphs 34
        Sensation vs. Feeling 39
        The Dhammas 42
    The Vipassana Perspective 43
    Refrain 45

Part Two
THE FOUR FOUNDATIONS OF ATTENTION
Sutta Study

1 Contemplation of Somatic Activities 51
    Sensations 52
        Satipatthāna Sutta: Contemplation of the Body 52
        Mindfulness of Breathing 52
    Meditation 57
    Matter 62
    Attention to Breathing 63
    Proprioception 68
    Interoception 69
    Physiological Activities 70
    The Elements 71
    The Dispersion of Matter 73
    In Summary 73

2 Contemplation of the Activities of Feeling 75
    Feeling 76
        Satipatthāna Sutta: Contemplation of Feeling 77
    From Sensations to Feelings 78
    Feelings as Cognitive Activity 79

The "I" and the "Proto-I" 80
Instinct and Habit..82
Innate or Acquired 84
Desire and Reaction...86
Back to the *Sutta*: The Mind-Body Connection 90
   Affective Valence..*93*
   Cause and Effect: Material and Mental Phenomena........*95*
Reflexes and Conditioning 97
Feelings: The Key to the Whole Process........................101
Immeasurable Affective States..103
In Summary..104

3 Contemplation of Activities of Knowing 105
Understanding Thoughts with the *Abhidhamma* 106
Knowing 107
   Satipatthāna Sutta: Contemplation of Consciousness.....*109*
Citta and Its Activities...110
Citta as the Building Block of Awareness.....................112
   Citta and the Seven Mental Processes *113*
Citta Process and Concepts 117
   Matter and Space..*118*
Conditioned Cognitive Activity 119
Sati is Cognitive Activity...122
Composite Phenomena and Ultimate Realities...........124
Contemplating the Concept of "I" 125
The Basis of the Mind and the Portal to the Mind.....127
Self-Transcendence..129
Mindfulness and the Memory of Oneself 131
   The Dimension of "Now"..*133*
   The "Present" in Dhamma *134*
   Working Memory and the Continuity Field *136*
Sati and Memory..140
   Primary Emotions *140*
   Secondary Emotions *141*
   The Three Poisons *141*
Memory and Perception..143
   Perception and Intention *145*
The Characteristics of a Free Mind................................146
In Summary..148

4 Contemplation of the Phenomena of Experience 149
Experience 152
    Satipatthāna Sutta: Contemplation of Mental States 152
The Flow of Experience 158
The Five Hindrances 160
    Understanding the Hindrances 162
    Maintaining Balance in the Face of Hindrances 164
    Staying Connected with Sati 166
    Working with the Hindrances 168
    Non-Attentive Activity and Sati 170
    Liberation from Hindrances 171
Sati and Transcendence 175
Awareness Without Object 178
    Latent Tendencies 179
Characteristics of Empty Awareness 180
Understanding of Truth 180
    Satipatthāna Sutta: Conclusion 183

Index 185

FOREWORD

We live in difficult times—the most dangerous time in human history, according to Noam Chomsky. What we do (or don't do) within the next few decades is likely to have great consequences not only for our species, but for the whole of the biosphere. So...what should we do? According to Chan (Zen) master Yunmen, the fruit of the spiritual path is simply that we learn to "respond appropriately." But what is an appropriate response to the greatest challenge humanity has ever faced?

When we consider the problems that Chomsky highlights—the climate crisis, nuclear weapons, the decline of democracy around the world—we naturally look for institutional responses that affect political and economic policies. But such a single-minded focus on systemic change overlooks something else important: individual transformation, of the sort that Buddhism has traditionally emphasized. As we have recently been reminded, democracies are fragile, relying on the maturity of informed citizens who support prosocial behavior. Rampant greed and consumerism are among the root problems behind our collective destruction of the planet's ecosystems. We need new values, new priorities, that not only acknowledge but cherish our nonduality with the earth, our mother as well as our home. What encourages the development of people who are less self-centered, more empathic, and compassionate? How do we become individuals who try to respond appropriately to the "polycrisis"?

The necessity for self-transformation today is the context for this book, which explains in precise detail the process whereby we can reconstruct ourselves. The foundational text is the *Satipatthana Sutta*, one of the most important early Buddhist suttas for its careful descriptions of psycho-spiritual meditative practices that can transform how we experience the world and how we live in it. Buddhism is usually understood as one of the main "world religions," but if religion is about a postmortem salvation, then the *"the Discourse on the Four Foundations of Mindfulness"* (to offer an expansive English translation of the title) focuses on something very different: not transcending this world but transcending our usual ways of experiencing it, including how we usually experience ourselves.

For this text, "awakening" is not about escaping life and physical rebirth but dispelling the delusion of a separate self whose wellbeing is separate from the wellbeing of others -- "others" including the manifold sibling species that co-create the biosphere with us. When "I" give up attachment and stop conceiving of myself as a discrete reality, the realization arises that subject and object are mutually constructed. "Forgetting oneself" (as Dogen puts it) allows absorption into the true reality of a boundless web of impermanent and interdependent processes that includes ourselves. This goes beyond the practice of mindfulness that has recently become popular: concentration does not by itself lead to liberation from the delusion of self with all its attendant stresses and anxieties. Attention is the doorway to true awareness and genuine insight. It is by contemplating the flow of experience that the self-other duality is resolved and enlightenment occurs, leading to a wisdom and serenity unperturbed by the unavoidable vicissitudes of daily life.

There are many translations of the *Satipatthana Sutta*, along with a growing number of commentaries on it. What is especially valuable about this version is that the original Pali text—over two thousand years old!—is explained with the help of modern Western psychology. The path of intuitive introspection that Buddhism has always taught, leading to insight into the nature of one's mind, is thereby synthesized with recent discoveries in cognitive neuroscience, including the neurology of consciousness itself. The objective "third person" focus of Western science, which emphasizes objectivity and replicability, supports the "first person" perspective of contemplative practices, and vice-versa.

Without diminishing the importance of this book, and the meditative exercises it explains so well, I think it is important to conclude by returning to Chomsky's concerns. The *Satipatthana Sutta* is about the transformative path of individuals. Today we certainly need that, perhaps more than ever, but we also need something else, something more: individuals on the path of liberation who also turn their attention to the multivalent social and ecological crises of our time, who are committed to responding appropriately insofar as they can.

The *bodhisattva path*, emphasized in Mahayana Buddhism, unites these concerns. Bodhisattvas have a double practice: they continue to work on their own personal transformation while also engaging in activities that contribute to the wellbeing of everyone. Often this has been understood as individuals helping other individuals, but today, given the institutional scale of the problems that face us, we also need to work together in various ways to address the processes by which important collective decisions are made. The bodhisattva path is arguably the most important teaching that Buddhism offers us today, and meditative practices that promote individual transformation—such as those outlined so well in the *Satipatthana Sutta* and explicated so well in the pages that follow—are an essential part of it.

David Loy, Buddhist teacher and author
September, 2023

PREFACE

This book is a product of many years of study, practice, and teaching of Vipassana meditation. It is an interdisciplinary text that interconnects the traditional Buddhist discourse with that of contemporary scientific psychology. This innovative approach led to intense debate at our Institute of Integral Psychology. Eventually, due to the interest generated both inside our small group and in international Spanish-speaking communities, some commentaries about the approach were published in Spanish, and later to a smaller readership in Basque.

However, we began to feel that these novel ideas needed to be broadcast on a larger stage. To this end, Andrew Molloy, a long-standing member of the sangha and collaborator at the Institute, suggested producing a much more comprehensive and complete synthesis, but this time in English. This book is the result. It required some fifteen months of cooperation between teacher and student, and is a product of numerous question-and-answer sessions, the last of which were online due to the health pandemic.

Even though this book includes a great deal of scientific knowledge, it is not, however, a scientific document, and this is why it is not accompanied by bibliographic references. It is an erudite book, but you do not need to know much Buddhism or psychology to be able to read it. Its reading requires calm and the possession of a contemplative capacity. It is intended to expound the rational and scientific arguments that allow us to understand "things as they really are." With this theoretical background, meditation practice will take care of the process of acceptance of human physical, affective, and cognitive limits.

Vipassana

Vipassana is a style of meditation that is characteristic of the Buddha—in fact, it is said to be what the Buddha used for his "awakening." It is a ritualized way of deliberately practicing those operations that a human organism carries out to mature psychologically. It is based on developing a type of conscious and constant meta-attention that we employ when learning a new skill or acquiring new knowledge. The development of this type of attention helps resolve cognitive distortions, as well as affective conflict or psychosomatic disorders. To summarize, Vipassana, the way we conceive and practice it, is a universal method to overcome psychological suffering and existential dissatisfaction.

This method is the unseen origin of the "key technique" of the "third generation cognitive-behavioral psychotherapies"—mindfulness. It is one of the most advanced tools at our disposal to treat psychological malaise. Mindfulness is the name used in our present-day cultural environment to refer an "acculturated" version of Satipatthāna, the "path to mindfulness," which was one of the last adaptations of the method used in the Buddha's teachings to achieve freedom from dissatisfaction.

Since the 1990s, there has been impressive growth in scientific knowledge about how the brain and the central nervous system function. This has provided physiological and electrochemical descriptions of the influence of meditation on somatic, emotional, and cognitive health. As a result, mindfulness has gained a social prestige that Vipassana and other contemplative practices never had, due to negative associations with belief systems, religion, and spirituality in general. Although arising from the area of mind/body medicine, associated research has developed in both neuroscience and psychology. The progress in understanding what it means to be a human being, provided by research into the effects of contemplative practices, has shaken the foundations of the philosophy of science and, in particular, of inquiry into consciousness.

To be able to explain the underlying mechanisms of Vipassana, new terms have been coined, or old terms have been adapted—for instance metacognition (Teasdale et al. 2002), decentering (Fresco et al. 2007), cognitive defusion (Fletcher and Hayes) or reperception (Shapiro et al. 2006). Likewise, constructs such as "mental perception," "mentalization," or "theory of mind" have all been affected by the auge of mindfulness.

In turn, the transmission and practice of Vipassana have been affected by these perspectives, which have arisen from an explosion of interest in mindfulness. Mindfulness has become a broad-spectrum psychopedagogical tool in use not only in the area of health—both physical and mental—but also education and industry. Furthermore, it has become a transdiagnostic and transtherapeutic instrument for psychosocial and mental health treatment.

This book aims to open a dialogue between these areas of knowledge, which will lead to an improved acceptance of the Buddha's method by those who have begun to practice "mindfulness" and who would like to extend their knowledge beyond managing psychological malaise or personal improvement on a path towards transcendence of existential dissatisfaction.

A profound influence on our approach to the Buddha's dharma is the work of David Loy. Our friend and teacher takes a reverse journey to what is normal among mindfulness practitioners. As a professor of philosophy, he uncovers in the dharma a method for achieving the good or full life that philosophical activity pursues. His work on nonduality was an introduction for those of us who came to the dharma from the western academic sphere. He showed us that the human drama is the experience of "lack," or existential dissatisfaction, which is characteristic of a mentality based upon the belief in the individual—the "I" as a measure of all things. David explains in graphic detail that the present situation of our "developed society" is due to the systematic concealment of the poisons (*kilesas* in Pali). These are typical characteristics of the dominant mentality of a supposedly civilized world, and include avarice, hate of anything different, and the illusion of individual happiness. It is precisely this realization that leads him to denounce the manipulation of the dharma in mindfulness as "McMindfulness," underlining the danger implicit in converting the Buddha's teachings into a mass market product dedicated to reinforcing the attachment to "oneself." His present-day teaching is oriented towards reunifying humans with their biological underpinnings and the environment.

The "I"

A central concept in Vipassana is contemplation of the "I." Used throughout the book, this term refers to a concept or mental construct that is almost inevitable for human beings (and, very likely, for other animals as well) to employ. When speaking, it is likewise inevitable, as it represents the speaker. This continuity, centrality, and apparent dominance of the subject over the experience leads us to believe that "I" is the agent that makes choices and decisions. This "oneself" generates an "identity," the belief that there is an "entity" with its very own existence that is separate from all other physical and mental objects.

The idea that "I am I" is self-evident, and because it is completely obvious, it's taken for granted. Therefore, it becomes an irrefutable truth and subject to rights and duties. The existence of the "I" not only is never doubted but has been the subject of reflection in philosophy, psychology, biology, anthropology, etc. Human knowledge is "egocentric"—"ego" coming from Latin and meaning "I."

This concept arises from the need to locate this "self" amongst all the objects in consciousness. The experience that there is a body that feels and interacts with other physical objects leads to the idea of a being that is separate and different from other objects. The experience of seeing oneself as an object, along with the continuity of that perception, gives rise to a memory. This continuity becomes time and so generates an autobiography. Consciousness is now divided between "me" and "not me."

The initial and precursory consciousness becomes dissociated in the human being precisely because of this identification with the "I." The separation between "I" and "the other" provokes existential anguish, a longing for unity. Unfortunately, reunification is impossible if one starts from this desire. From here, duality explodes into a thousand pieces. In Western philosophical tradition, the subject was tied to the "knot of the world"; the body is in the mind and the mind is in the body. This philosophy becomes a type of competition between two teams, each pulling on one end of the rope as they search for original consciousness in the body or in the mind.

Materialism continues to believe that just as soon as matter is fully known, then reunion with consciousness will occur. Idealism lost all credibility by having to resort to a divine authority from which the body and individual consciousness both arise. This "self" has very powerful instinctive impulses that desire to be dominated through moral norms that protect coexistence. What is more, the cyclical nature of human life—being born, maturing, aging, and dying—means that the "self" is subject to an evolutionary process of which it is totally ignorant. This "I" is the result, therefore, of the minimum part that it is capable of understanding or managing the complex biological, affective, and cognitive processes that constitute it.

In the Buddha's method, this belief in a unique, central, permanent, and sovereign "I"—that is to say, the refusal to recognize the impermanence of it (as well as our dependence on it)—produces an enormous burden of ignorance and dissatisfaction.

The Integral Perspective

We believe it important to define for the reader exactly what we mean by "Integral." Although the main aim of the book is to integrate different strands of developing knowledge concerning the practice of Vipassana meditation, we primarily use this term from the body of work by Ken Wilber. Those who already know about Wilber's "Integral vision" will recognize many of the classifications and distinctions we use to organize the phenomenology of the meditative process. Wilber is one of our fundamental influences. He must be credited with having clearly organized the immense amount of information written or otherwise transmitted over the centuries about the human phenomenon. Successive versions of his theory have enriched our world view, as well as our understanding of the processes and phenomena that occur during our meditation practice.

As we see it, Wilber moved from transpersonal psychology to elaborating his Integral Theory when he realized that mystical experiences did not appear at the highest level of psychological development, as had been assumed by transpersonal psychology, but rather at every level. Psychological development works by levels and corresponds to psychological maturation, while mystical experiences are states of consciousness, not levels.

These had been explored by mystics of different persuasions and are generally organized into states: waking, dreaming, dreamless, and non-dual sleep.

This distinction was key to our understanding of "The Four Foundations of Mindfulness." We distinguish between the first three "foundations"—which are practiced especially, but not exclusively, with an orientation towards psychological maturation—and the fourth, which affects spiritual awakening. What today are generally considered attentional and generative or instructive meditations spring from the first three, while the deconstructive meditations emerged from the fourth.

When meditating, this distinction may not be obvious—especially at the beginning—but the more one practices, the more one realizes. In dharma terms, this is viewed as the balance between *Samatha* (calm, tranquility) and Vipassana. (See Figure 1.)

Samatha	Vipassana
Attention with object	**Attention without object**
Physical feelings Affects Cognitions	Attention to the flow of experience, the emergence and cessation of phenomena
Psychological Maturation	**Spiritual Awakening**
Constructive and generative practices: • Observation of the object • Observation of the relationship • Observation of the subject	Deconstructive practices: • Observation of the phenomena • Observation of the relationships • Observation of the observer

Figure 1: The typology of meditation practice.

There is a key element in this whole process—"perspicacity," or the ability to realize what was missed. It is not only "metaconsciousness" but rather a widened vision that allows ever more subtle aspects of "agency" to become objects to be operated upon. It appears that perspicacity and attachment are good predictors of the difficulty and consequent speed of progress that the meditator will encounter on the "path." These two elements have relevant parallels which Wilber calls "clean up" and "show up."

Vipassana affects the four quadrants of the "Wilberian" model. Although it is in itself a technology of the inner/individual quadrant—a "technology of the self" in Foucault's terms, implying work that the subject itself carries out on its subjective world—Vipassana also has effects on physiological health (outer/individual quadrant), as has been proven by science. And, it exerts an undeniable influence on the social sphere (outer/collective quadrant), as shown by its implementation in work and education settings, as well as on the cultural arena (inner/collective quadrant). It thereby exerts an undeniable influence over the dominant mentality, which can clearly be seen in contemporary philosophy of science.

Another key element of Wilber's AQAL model (all quadrants, all levels, all lines, all states, and all types) is the level of development. In the Sutta, this evolutionary process can be seen in the first three "foundations." The meditator develops the three basic evolutionary aspects: somatic-sensory, affective-emotional, and cognitive-moral. In this last can be found the development of faith or spirituality.

Nevertheless, the fourth foundation is an immersion in the flow of experiencing continually changing states of consciousness. Vipassana is all about witnessing the arising and ceasing of phenomena and discovering the causal link that joins them. When we meditate, we try to discover the order that is implicit in the bewildering flow of phenomena. Thus, we realize the need for a certain mental stability. Perspicacity leads to calm, and calm leads to perspicacity. Meditation leads to understanding and controlling all the obstacles to calm: agitation or disconnection, cognitive, affective, and somatic. This process gives us insight into the causal relationships between physical sensation and desire, perception and conditioning, or cognitive structures and consciousness.

Advances have come from the game of "include and transcend." This refers to the way one progresses in any of the four spheres of experience. It starts from an imbalance or a conflict between two elements, and then polarity is worked upon until, when balance is achieved, one can "include and transcend."

We wish to underline the metaphysical dimension. We believe that one of the roots of the collective malaise is the prevailing metaphysical materialism. As Wilber points out, the Enlightenment implanted a "flattened" view of the world. Even if it was necessary at that particular time to overcome the superstitions and divine laws that the dominant systems of government had employed, the deleterious effect this produced on all of our minds—this reduction to matter of anything that has its own existence—has caused an unprecedented ecological and psychological disturbance. Philosophy of Science has been advancing towards a more idealistic metaphysics, with a more Eastern flavor, as demonstrated by the panpsychic or cosmopsychistic theories that have been in vogue in recent years.

It must be said, however, that Wilber's influence on this book is more in what is unseen than in what we have mentioned. To set out on the path of Vipassana meditation is, for us, a comprehensive approach to the human phenomenon.

Other Influences

Given that the aim of this book is to be a reference for those practicing Vipassana, not a textbook, we have eschewed quotations or bibliographical references. Notwithstanding, it is correct to acknowledge the particular influence of certain authors whose ideas or words may be glimpsed in the text.

Basic Psychology

Michael Posner's theory of the three attention networks is a crucial element for we see attention as a key cognitive activity in the Buddha's method. His theory of the three networks explains the psychological key to the Buddha's method. *Vayama* is the alertness level of the system, *samadhi* the orientation network, and *sati* the executive network. These parallels are beginning to be acknowledged by some authors investigating the neuroscience of mindfulness.

> Note that the term Samadhi is used in two different ways in this book. Samadhi with a capital letter refers to the psychological block of the Noble Eightfold Path as a whole and that encompasses sati, samadhi and vayama. However, when we mention samadhi in all lower case, we are referring to a type of attention that is able to maintain a single phenomenon under its focus.

Affective Neuroscience and Neuropsychoanalysis

Likewise, Jaak Panksepp's "affective neuroscience" contributes the nested structure that allows us to order the three classes of activities—somatic, affective, and cognitive. Panksepp proposes that human beings—as is the case with other sentient beings who are "affective"—are driven by subcortical structures that he calls "intentions-in-action," and by cortical structures that are "intentions-of-action." Primary emotional processes, which arise from subcortical structures, coordinate with secondary-process learning and memory mechanisms which occur in the basal ganglia. Both of these then interact with higher mental processes, which can exert a variety of top-down influences on the regulation of affects and emotions.

Neurophenomenology

The neurophenomenology of Francisco J. Varela, with its enactive position and embodiment philosophy, allows us to surmount those reductionisms that relegate the cognitive to some sort of exclusively rational, individualized, abstract, and incorporeal mechanism, thereby providing us with the guidelines to approach "experience in the first person"—experience as it happens moment by moment.

Cognitive Neuroscience

There are three authors who have had a profound influence on our perspective.

Amishi Jha has conducted research on attention, working memory, mindfulness, and the neural bases of executive functioning and mental training. Her research has focused on the method by which attention selects information as relevant or irrelevant, as well as how working memory then allows that information to be manipulated. Her contribution has been essential to understanding the complex role of attention in meditation.

Dave Vago is author of the S-ART framework—the most integrative proposal in modern mindfulness. It includes self-transcendence, which from our perspective is what makes the practice of sati the ideal tool to develop wisdom.

Dhamma

Our main reference for the *Dhamma* is Gil Fronsdal, from whom we have learned to respect the history and development of Buddhism in the West. We also share his vision for Vipassana meditation. *Note that our use of "Dhamma" with an initial capital refers to Buddha's teachings, whereas "dhamma" in lower case means knowledge gained through direct experience.*

Ethics

Tara Brach also combines Western psychology and Eastern spiritual practices. She contributes a forgotten element to modern mindfulness—ethics. It is an important part of meditation, as the Buddha's method is, in itself, psychoethical. We have gained from Tara a full and compassionate commitment to our world.

Insight

Last, but by no means least, we must acknowledge our debt to Andrea Grabovac, whose work we follow with great interest. Andrea is the author who has stayed the most faithful to the Vipassana model inside the modern mindfulness movement. Her contributions on the "mechanisms of mindfulness" and "Vipassana insights" have been extremely influential on our Integral Vipassana approach.

Of course, there are many more authors and teachers in this book. We cannot, however, mention them all in this preface, nor is it our intention to overload the text with "erudite" references that might well do more to confuse than to clarify. We are naturally extremely indebted to them all.

A Companion on the Road

This book was conceived to be a kind of travel companion. The Buddha's road is not an easy one. The journey requires a transformation of the conventional perspective on health, emotions, mind, and the meaning of life. This conventional perspective is powerful—without altering it, one cannot expect to overcome on their own all the obstacles to mental stability and erroneous conceptions that separate us from happiness and wisdom.

In the Therevada tradition, "the school of the pioneers," the figure of a "spiritual friend," the *"kalyāṇa-mitta,"* is propounded instead of a "teacher" figure. This companion on the road is the person who is most experienced and skillful in the quest for ever higher degrees of freedom. Nowadays, the figure of the old-style teacher either no longer exists or is very hard to find. This book has been conceived to offer replies and wisdom to the questions and doubts that arise as practitioners encounter inevitable difficulties on the road.

This text is a dialogue about the practice—from how to tackle postural questions and being physically uncomfortable, to managing emotions and unpleasant states of mind, to developing metaconscious work habits that allow you to overcome cognitive blocks and phases of stagnation or boredom. You will also find concrete descriptions of the processes you undergo, as well as explanations of how the mind works.

Instead of referring to complex and occasionally cryptic Buddhist literature, this text gives descriptions and explanations springing from a Western mentality. What may originally appear to be mythic beliefs or superstitions are put into a rational and scientific context. Furthermore, where modernity and postmodernity can advance no more, the interpretation of the *Dhamma* we offer leads to a transcendental philosophical vision that overcomes rationality and relativism.

Our book will not only help you reflect on philosophical and existential questions, it will provide you with a fresh, joyous, and loving vision of the human phenomenon.

We sincerely hope it is so.

PART ONE

BUDDHISM, VIPASSANA, AND OUR WORLD

INTRODUCTION

The aim of this work is to present one of the most important teachings of Buddha's worldview, *The Discourse on the Four Foundations of Mindfulness*. This discourse is important because it is a concise (yet also very precise) account of his meditation technique. In this introduction, we place Buddha's figure in historical context and look at how his teaching has been transmitted down to us.

Buddha and His Time

The Buddha (The Awakened One) was an historical figure by the name of Siddhattha Gotama. Born in what we know today as Nepal, he lived in the north of India between the fifth and sixth centuries BCE. Not much is known about his life, mainly because he directed all his followers' attention towards his teaching while at the same time warning them of the risks of a personality cult. Born into a family of gentry in northern India, tradition says that he experienced existential angst when he became aware that disease, aging, and death are the universal destiny of human beings. As a result, he decided to find a way to resolve the dissatisfaction that is inherent to being human. For several years, he put into practice the most sophisticated mystical techniques of his time. He was a disciple to teachers and yogis of high standing, adopting the most extreme asceticism—all in search of liberation from this dissatisfaction.

Unlike other spiritual leaders who considered themselves divine or omniscient, the Buddha always presented himself as a human being, and his method was intended to be universally applicable. He neither claimed a privileged relationship with any god, nor did he represent a chosen people. He lived in an era that was the climax of Brahmanism (the religion based on the authority of the Brahmins or priests), and the spiritual environment was dominated by the *Vedas*, the first known writings of India, with their essentially poetic, ritual, and esoteric content. Brahmanism was based on the ritual consumption of *soma* (a psychotropic drug) and on extremely complex public and ritualized sacrifices of hundreds of animals, which were carried out by the Brahmin priests. Only the very highest in society (priests, dignitaries, and warriors) could participate in these ceremonies. In this context, there arose several movements rejecting the religiosity and exotic ceremonies implicit in the *Vedas*, and reacting against the authority of the Brahmin priests.

A new culture began to develop, possibly linked to the world of artisans and merchants, and led by dissident Brahmins and sages of all types who endorsed more flexible and participatory forms of life and governance. It is the era in which the *Upanishads* (the mystical section of the *Vedas*) were transmitted, and new dissident traditions appeared, such as Jainism. The *Upanishads* are probably based on the mystical experiences of people who, tired of the official ritualistic religion, withdrew to the forests to live as ascetics or hermits, and there found ways to internalize sacrifice. They met to hear the words of other spiritual teachers and to discuss the divine, and later spread their ideas.

An Era of Transformation

Hindu philosophical traditions are classified heuristically as either orthodox or heterodox, *astika* or *nastika*, depending on whether or not they accept the authority of the *Vedas*. Vedism is based on an extremely complex sacrificial structure controlled by priestly families and open only to the "noble" or *arya* society—that is to say, the most dominant classes of society. The tradition of the Buddha must be considered heterodox because he does not accept the idea of a soul transiting from one existence to another as it seeks a better reincarnation. Buddha did not recognize the authority of the Brahmins, nor did he believe that birth into a particular class or caste was fundamental for spiritual progress. Any person—man or woman—who followed his method could free himself or herself from suffering.

The Buddha's method does not seek liberation in outer experience, but rather in inner experience. From his perspective, suffering arises because we cannot accept certain inevitabilities: that we are born without choosing to do so, that we will fall ill, that we will age, that we will die. We also suffer because we cannot always attain what we wish for, and we can always lose what we have. These things happen because we live in ignorance and are tied to it by unconscious conditioning.

Buddha taught that in order to escape ignorance and transcend this suffering, human beings need to behave ethically, understand how the mind works, and train it through meditation.

The Buddha lived in an historical context that involved a great transformation of the human mentality, comparable to that of the modern scientific revolution. This was an era, sometimes termed *axial*, when humans became aware of themselves and their limitations, and so began to seek salvation. This search was guided by introspection and reflection, which also lead to arguments over who was right. Out of these controversies arose the principal currents of thought and spirituality that continue to this day. There were five main geographical strands: China (Confucianism and Taoism), India (Hinduism and Buddhism), Persia (Zoroastrianism), Israel (monotheism), and Greece (philosophy).

Scripture and Pali

The first centuries BCE saw the shift from oral to written transmission. History, strictly speaking, begins with writing. Religion, which at that time was the social glue, was utterly transformed by this shift. When religious texts are written down, they tend to become imbued with a larger dimension of authority, rather than when they are transmitted orally, which is based on memory. Most religions (Judaism, Christianity, Islam, Buddhism, Jainism,

Sikhism, Confucianism, Taoism, etc.) tend to resort to sacred scriptures to codify both the will of their founders and the higher truths of their "revelation."

However, not all sacred texts have the same authority. There are differences between texts with maximum authority and those with no authority—authority can even vary between different versions of the same text. This is what is known as the canonization process, in which the chosen texts purport to transmit universal and valid truths about the greatest of matters. This must be borne in mind when interpreting the Buddhist canon.

Canons such as the Confucian, the Taoist, the Eastern Buddhist, the Avesta, the Hebrew Bible, or recensions of Greek "classics" in the West, date from the period between 200 BCE and 200 CE—in the case of Buddhism, more than two centuries after the death of the historical Buddha.

The first written evidence of the existence of Buddhism originates from the time of King Ashoka, who ruled the Maurya kingdom in the north of India from 269 to 232 BCE. The inscriptions of King Ashoka are written in a *prakrita* language. The English word "prakrit" comes from the Sanskrit *prākrita* (meaning 'original, natural, normal, ordinary, usual,') which may be interpreted as vernacular, in contrast with religious and literary Sanskrit. The term Prakrit refers to a group of different languages spoken in ancient India. While Sanskrit was a cultured language used by Brahmins (priests) in religious rituals, Prakrit was the means of spreading heterodox beliefs such as Jainism (in Maharashtri) or Buddhism (in Pali).

Ashoka issued edicts, which were then translated into various Prakrit languages and then disseminated throughout his kingdom. Scholars concur that the oldest Buddhist texts are those written in Pali, although the Buddhist scriptures have become a vast body of texts written in many diverse Asian languages.

Pali was considered by early Buddhists to be linguistically similar to ancient *Magadhi*—or even to be a direct descendant of that language—and was therefore very likely the language used by the Buddha. The scriptures of Theravada Buddhism, the oldest school of Buddhism still existent today, had previously been transmitted orally and were first written down in Pali during the first century BCE.

T.W. Rhys Davids, the first Western translator of Pali, suggested that Pali might have originated as some sort of *lingua franca*, or language of communication, for the educated laity, and that it was used at the time of the Buddha. However, most modern scholars believe that Pali evolved over many centuries, only becoming fixed when the Pali Canon was put in writing in Sri Lanka. In India, it would finally be replaced by Sanskrit as the dominant literary and religious language.

The work of Buddhaghosa in the fifth century CE was hugely important in the resurgence of Pali as an academically important language in Buddhist thinking. The commentaries that Buddhaghosa wrote (including the *Visuddhimagga*, the most influential Buddhist meditation manual) codified and condensed the tradition of commentary, which had long been preserved in Sri Lanka.

These days, Pali is studied mainly to be able to directly access the oldest Buddhist scriptures, though it is also used in recitations in ritual contexts. In Southeast Asia today, Pali is a sacred language in the same way as ecclesiastical Latin is in Western Europe. Buddhist monks still compose texts in Pali and use this language as a *lingua franca* in Myanmar, Sri Lanka, and Thailand, where the great centers of Pali learning are also to be found.

Since the nineteenth century, a number of societies have dedicated themselves to promoting studies in Pali around the world. The Maha Bodhi Society, founded by Anagarika Dhammapala, is perhaps the one which has been most active in preserving and advancing information about the language and its literature. In Europe, the Pali Text Society, based in the United Kingdom, has been a key promoter of the study of Pali by Western scholars since its foundation in 1881. The Royal Library of Denmark is the institution that owns the major collections of Pali manuscripts.

The Councils and the Pali Canon

Although we do not know the exact date, sometime after the Buddha's death, a council was held to establish the monastic norms, doctrines, and practices that he had taught. There was still no use of a writing system, though the monks were accustomed to memorizing a great deal of information by employing sophisticated mnemonic methods. They adopted a style, based on formulas and repetition, which is still preserved in the written *suttas* (speeches) today. They would recite them in verse, and it is very likely they also sang these *suttas* so as to better memorize them.

Approximately a hundred years later, a second council was held where it became apparent that each group had a different interpretation of the doctrines and practices that they remembered. This council witnessed the first schism within Buddhism, a split that had important historical consequences that continue to this day. A trend towards the idealization and deification of the figure of the Buddha began. The ancestors of what is today Mahayana Buddhism viewed all of the acts of the Buddha since his birth as being immaculate—they believed he had never known a single moment of desire, hatred, or ignorance, even before his "awakening." This affirmation presupposed that nobody would really ever be able to reach "true awakening" and that the Buddha was a transcendental being and not an ordinary man. This turned his *dhamma*, his teachings, into a standard religion and a closed belief system, so stripping it of its greatest virtue—the promise that any person who follows the method honestly, with insight and perseverance, may be freed of suffering. This tension has been explained as being between an "innatist" Mahayana and a "constructivist" Theravada.

Due to the difficulty of memorizing the colossal corpus of teachings, the monks started to specialize. There were "reciters of long discourses," "reciters of medium-length discourses," and so on. This was the structure that was taken as a base and which, more or less, has been maintained until today.

As it is said that the Buddha spoke of his teaching as the "path" and of the norms for monastic life as "discipline," the texts were divided between the discourses, or *suttas*; the norms for the monks, or *vinaya*; and a third group composed of an assortment of teachings. The *suttas*, in turn, were divided into four blocks: the long, the medium length, the grouped (by themes), and the numerical (which spoke of elements that were organized into pairs, groups of three, four, and even up to eleven).

One hundred years later, a third council promoted by King Ashoka took up the work of correcting misinterpretations and began to develop the *Abhidhamma*, an extraordinarily detailed analysis of the principles that govern physical and mental processes. This eventually constituted the third part of the *Tipitaka* or Pali Canon. Thanks to Ashoka, the Buddha's teachings were introduced into Sri Lanka, where they would be long preserved. With the objective of protecting the teachings from possible losses, whether due to invasion or famine, the Sinhalese monks for the first time wrote down all the remembered texts on palm leaves. The texts, which were written in the first century BCE, were kept in different baskets—*Vinaya, Suttas, Abhidhamma*—which is why this canon is considered as the most reliable transcription in the Pali language of the Buddha's teaching, and is known as *Tipitaka*, the "Three Baskets."

During the reign of Emperor Ashoka, the Sarvastivada school also diverged from the mainstream. According to the Theravada school, after the textual interpretation implemented by the council, the emperor dispatched missions to introduce Buddhism into new regions both within his empire and beyond. These included what is today Pakistan, the present-day southeast of Afghanistan, Southern India, Sri Lanka and Burma. Other traditions do not view this council the same way the Theravada school does.

After the death of Emperor Ashoka, the Sarvastivada school was introduced into Kashmir. From there, it spread to present-day Afghanistan. Around the year 190 BCE, the Darmagupta school spread into what are today Pakistan, Afghanistan, Iran, Central Asia, and even China. The Chinese adopted the Darmaguptaka version of the vows of the monks and the nuns. Over the centuries, this version of the monastic discipline rules was transmitted to Korea, Japan, and Vietnam.

Both the Theravada and Sarvastivada schools held their own fourth council. The first was convened in the year 83 CE in Sri Lanka. In order to preserve authenticity, the Buddha's teachings were written down in the

Pali language for the first time. This became the first version of the *Tipitaka* or Pali Canon. Nevertheless, the other schools continued to transmit the teachings orally, and each expressed its own position on many points of instruction in the *Abhidamma* basket.

Meanwhile, the political situation in northern India, Kashmir, and Afghanistan experienced major developments. The Kushán dynasty, which lasted until the year 226 CE, spread out from present-day Tajikistan, Uzbekistan, Afghanistan, and Pakistan, through Kashmir and northwestern India, into central India. It joined the "Silk Road" to the mouth of the Indus River and thus allowed Buddhism to contact other cultures. And so, via this flow of ideas, did Buddhism enter China.

Around the same time, the Sarvastivada school held its fourth council in Kashmir. The council codified its own *Abhidhamma* and supervised the translation into Sanskrit of the "Three Baskets."

Between the fourth and fifth centuries CE, the *Mulasarvastivada* school split away from the mainstream of Kashmir. Towards the end of the eighth century CE, the Tibetans adopted their own version of the *Vinaya* which, in later centuries, spread from Tibet to Mongolia and into some regions of Russia.

No more councils were held until 1871 in Mandalay, Burma (present-day Myanmar). On this occasion King Mindón ordered that the Pali Canon be inscribed on 729 marble tablets that surrounded a pagoda, the Kuthodaw Pagoda, called by some "the world's largest book."

In 1954, six years after Burma's independence from the United Kingdom, the religious and lay leaders of Theravada Buddhism decided to hold the Sixth Buddhist Council in order to commemorate the 2,500 years since the Buddha's death. Monks from different countries with a Theravada tradition, as well as Buddhists from all over the world, attended this council. As at previous gatherings, his teachings were recited, and as a result, a new edition of the Pali Canon, including its commentaries, sub-commentaries, and other associated material, was published. This edition, called the Edition of the Sixth Council, is considered to be the most authoritative amongst the existing editions of Buddhist texts in the Theravada tradition.

We have made this journey through history to demonstrate that the texts of the Pali Canon, despite being the most authoritative of the Buddhist tradition, have suffered many vicissitudes and are not accepted by all the schools of Buddhism. They claim to be the literal words of the Buddha; however, we know nothing of the monks who originally compiled and then corrected them, time and time again, both during the 500 years of oral transmission and later the 2000 years of written transmission. There is no way of distinguishing authentic history and sermons from those that were invented. Today, confusion persists over the connection between *Pali* and the language of the ancient kingdom of Magadha. In brief, we do not have enough information to satisfy the criteria of scientific historiography.

> **This is a mythical story that should be interpreted from a symbolic point of view, and not literally.**

The Pali Canon includes literature that covers all areas of human life and addresses everybody, regardless of their cultural background or intellectual development. Sometimes it violates logic, falls into obvious contradictions, or speaks of supernatural stories that are not feasible from a rational or scientific point of view. In other words, this is a mythical story that should be interpreted from a symbolic point of view, and not literally. Even so, there is no doubt that the Buddhist worldview can be viewed as one of the oldest, most coherent, and most widespread in the world. As with all mythical stories, what is most essential in it is not its rationality or credibility. The continual revision and reinterpretation of the texts is an added value rather than a hermeneutical problem.

Enter Vipassana Meditation

Mahasi Sayadaw (1904-1982) set the stage for what we now know as the "Vipassana movement." This movement aims to provide lay people a type of meditation that has no need of monastic life for its development. Mahasi was a key figure in the Sixth Council. In fact, "Sayadaw" is the term used in Burma, modern Myanmar, to designate the abbot of a temple, or a monk with authority. The Council lasted from 1954 to 1956, and its ending coincided with the 2,500th anniversary of the Buddha's death. As with the other Buddhist councils, the main objective was to preserve the teachings and practices of the Buddha (the *Dhamma*), as they are understood in the Theravada tradition.

Throughout these two years, monks from different countries recited the Pali Canon and associated post-canonical literature. As a result, the council drafted a new version of the Pali texts. In total, 2,500 monks came from eight countries: Burma, Thailand, Cambodia, Laos, Vietnam, Sri Lanka, India, and Nepal. A temple in Japan also sent delegates. The only western monks who participated were Nyanatiloka and Nyanaponika Thera, born in Germany but living in Sri Lanka. Mahasi Sayadaw was appointed to ask questions about the *Dhamma*, a crucial role within the Council. His task was to raise doubts about the teaching which might affect the interpretation of the texts. Furthermore, Mahasi was the final editor of the Sixth Council.

Mahasi had a significant impact on the teaching of Vipassana (insight) meditation in the West and all throughout Asia. His practice style was based on the so-called "New Burmese Method" developed by Mingun Sayadaw (1868-1955), his meditation teacher. The new method was founded on the practice of meditation as described in the *Satipatthāna Sutta* (Discourse on the Four Foundations of Mindfulness). *Sati* meditation (mindfulness or conscious attention) implies the understanding of the three characteristics of existence: *Dukkha* (dissatisfaction), *Anatta* (non-self), and *Anicca* (impermanence). This is the only path to the understanding of *Paticca-samuppada* causality (dependent origination), the significant insight that leads to "Buddhahood" (awakening from illusion).

The New Burmese Method became popular among the laity in the 1950s. Although today we believe that Buddhism and meditation go hand in hand and can even be considered the same thing, most Buddhists at the time had dismissed the practice of meditation and had reduced Buddhism to a moral ideology, the ritual repetition of the teachings, and a way to acquire "good Karma" through generosity. Meditation was not a common practice in Buddhist societies, and this remains largely true today.

Many Buddhists, including monks, understand that they cannot "awake" without faithful meditation practice, but they are convinced that one can live a valuable and authentic Buddhist life without meditating. Many even think that meditation is inappropriate for this degenerate era, except for those few who live isolated from the world.

As in most cultures, spirituality has become institutionalized—that is to say, it has been reduced to religion, understood as a system of beliefs and rituals, and controlled by a hierarchical organization that claims to hold and/or lead to the correct relationship with the transcendent.

It was lay people who, as an attempt at resistance to the Western cultural invasion, began to be involved in the preservation and practice of meditation, which was in grave danger of disappearing.

The common belief was that anybody who wanted to practice meditation had to begin by first developing deep states of concentration called *jhanas*. However, achieving these sublime states of concentration required long periods of time retired from the world, as well as intensive practice.

A renewed interest by Burmese youth in meditation led some teachers such as Mingun, also known as U Narada, to develop a type of training adapted to the mentality that arose from the meeting of East and West. The message, which quickly spread, was that it was no longer necessary to spend long periods of isolation in the jungle or in a cave. Meditation was possible in a city.

Mingun promoted "deep vision meditation" based on "moment-by-moment concentration." At the beginning of the 20th century, Mingun was looking for a meditation system that offered direct access to "awakening" without the need to be a Buddhist scholar, and without the encumbrance of added norms or rituals. He travelled widely through Burma, interviewing monks, hermits, and sages.

Figure 2 shows the emergence of the "Vipassana Movement" and its most influential representatives, set within the long history of the Buddha tradition.

Integral Vipassana

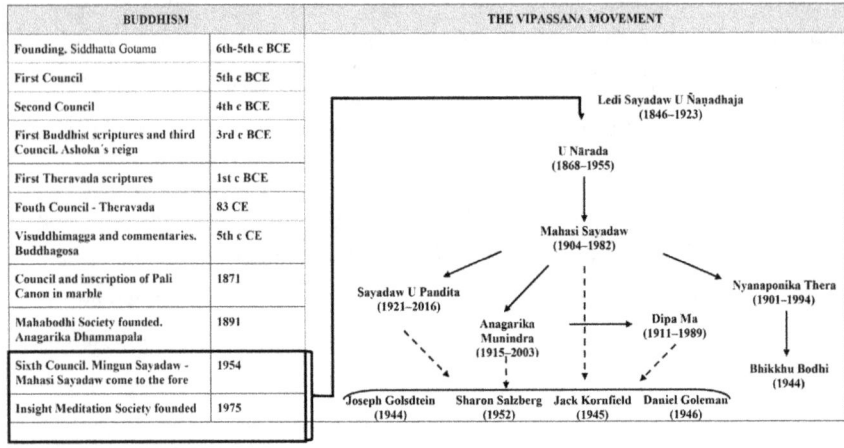

BUDDHISM	
Founding. Siddhatta Gotama	6th-5th c BCE
First Council	5th c BCE
Second Council	4th c BCE
First Buddhist scriptures and third Council. Ashoka's reign	3rd c BCE
First Theravada scriptures	1st c BCE
Fouth Council - Theravada	83 CE
Visuddhimagga and commentaries. Buddhagosa	5th c CE
Council and inscription of Pali Canon in marble	1871
Mahabodhi Society founded. Anagarika Dhammapala	1891
Sixth Council. Mingun Sayadaw - Mahasi Sayadaw come to the fore	1954
Insight Meditation Society founded	1975

Figure 2: The Vipassana Movement refers to the reforms that occurred in Buddhism after the Sixth Council.

Vipassana Gains Traction

Mahasi became the main driver behind the Vipassana movement. The German monk Nyanaponika Thera, a disciple of Mahasi's, wrote *The Heart of Buddhist Meditation*, a modern spiritual classic and the most cited book on meditation of all time, which includes a complete translation of *Satipatthāna*. Bhikkhu Bodhi, one of the most renowned Buddhist authorities of our times, was a student of Nyanaponika's. The first Western Vipassana teachers studied under Asian masters who were part of this Vipassana movement of the twentieth century: Joseph Goldstein studied with Mahasi and his students Anagarika Munindra and U Pandita; Sharon Salzberg studied with Goenka, Mahasi, Munindra, and U Pandita; Jack Kornfield studied with *Ajahn* Cha and Mahasi Sayadaw; and Goleman studied with Sayadaw U Pandita. (*Ajahn* is the form of address for important monks in Thailand.)

While Zen and Tibetan Buddhism came to the West via Asian masters who were usually monks, Vipassana came via Westerners who, after a few years as monks in Asia, returned home as lay teachers. The Vipassana movement in the West has always been secular and, in that sense, has transformed the traditional monastic form of Theravada Buddhism, whence it emerged. Even *Ajahn* Dhiravamsa and *Ajahn* Sobin, two of the Thai meditation teachers who have been most successful in the West, gave up the robe shortly after arriving in England and the United States, respectively.

The bestselling book *Emotional Intelligence* by Daniel Goleman is one of the most acclaimed of recent times. However, Vipassana teachings, which were the main inspiration for the book, are not mentioned anywhere in it. Goleman himself stated in another of his books that "the Dharma was so disguised that it could never be proved before a judge." His Vipassana master, U Pandita, a disciple of Mahasi, has used the term "SQ" (Spiritual Quotient), to refer to the insights and practical tools that modern Vipassana provides. Goleman himself accepted that SQ was the key to EQ, Emotional Quotient, affirming that "the key to EQ is 'self-awareness,'" and he thought that Vipassana provides us with this skill in the most profound way.

In a book subsequent to his successful *Full Catastrophe Living*, Jon Kabat-Zinn has also admitted that mindfulness was a "disguised" way of introducing the practice of Vipassana into American society. As Kabat-Zinn himself explained in an interview in *Time* magazine in 2012, "I started meditating myself when I was 22, in 1966, when I was a graduate student. Almost no one I knew was meditating back then and anyone who was, was considered to be somewhat beyond the lunatic fringe, a drug-crazed hippy communist."

Most Westerners trained in modern Vipassana have very little connection with the Theravada tradition. In fact, most Western meditators dedicated to Vipassana identify themselves as being practitioners of meditation and not as students or devotees of Theravada Buddhism. This meditation movement is devoted to knowledge and transcendence of oneself as a strategy to awaken, but it is not interested in the doctrinal, ritual, faith, and monastic elements of Theravada Buddhism.

It is not that there are two different forms of meditation—*Samatha* and Vipassana—but rather that some schools had made *Samatha* a requirement, when the Buddha's method actually required both. The Vipassana movement arose to restore the therapeutic and inquiring potential of meditation that the Buddha had discovered. The development of *sati*, constant conscious awareness, allows access to those processes that underlie subjectivity, which is its therapeutic value, while the therapeutic potential of *samadhi* is that it strengthens the focus of attention. Being able to use the tools of scientific psychology to observe and measure the effects of mindfulness practice has allowed this ancient method to become truly relevant in the modern world.

There are two distinguishing features of the Vipassana movement: first, the understanding that Buddhist *Samadhi* (mental stability) is the product of balanced effort (*vayama*) of constant conscious awareness (*sati*) and focused attention (*samadhi*); and second, the recognition that the path of *sati* described in the *Satipatthāna Sutta* is the most direct way to "awakening" (*nibbana*).

Both points have been the cause of much debate in the Buddhist world. Some authors have referred to this movement as "*vipassanavada*." The suffix "vada" refers not only to the doctrine but also to the school which follows this doctrine. It is somewhat similar to the suffix "-ism" used in English and refers to a series of beliefs which align it with a school of thought. It would, therefore, be a type of "vipassanism." There are even authors who hold that meditation with *sati* was already a practice before the Buddha and so would not be its distinguishing element.

The States of Absorption

Many Buddhist schools first teach *samatha* (concentration) before practicing Vipassana (deep vision). With this premise it is necessary to complete several states of absorption, or states of concentration, called *jhanas*.

The *jhanas* are states of consciousness where the separation between subject and object eventually disappears. This may happen accidentally or be induced through different means. The term *jhana* particularly refers to those states that occur during the meditative process and are classified depending on the degree of unity of the physical and mental processes that is achieved, and the stability of the experience. In the Buddha's tradition, there are four material *jhanas* and four immaterial ones. In the former, the state of consciousness becomes more purified as the degree of attachment to the sensual experience is balanced, until it reaches equanimity. In the latter, the experience is completely abstract since the somatic and affective activities have stopped.

According to these schools, in order to access these states of absorption, one has to develop fixed concentration (*appana samadhi*), a trance state where subject-object separation disappears. To access the first *jhana*, only a lower level of preliminary concentration (*upacara samadhi*) is needed. For the followers of the Vipassana movement, a type of momentary concentration (*khanika samadhi*) has to be developed, different from the above-mentioned. This type of concentration does not require absorption because that would impede constant conscious awareness (*sati*) from being present in the origination and cessation of the phenomena.

The twelve masters presented in Jack Kornfield's *Living Dharma* were probably the greatest Buddhist meditation teachers of the twentieth century. They wrote or clearly stated that one can practice Vipassana relying only on *khanika samadhi*. Of course, the path of the *jhanas* or meditative absorptions is not negated, but it is believed that with moment-by-moment concentration the five obstacles that impede mental stability can be overcome. This is another way to say that Buddhist *Samadhi* not only requires concentration (*samadhi*) but also *sati* and *vayama*. Some of these teachers have been monks since they were children and are erudite as well as being experienced meditators. They have studied the *Tipitaka*, the commentaries and sub-commentaries in the original Pali, and can therefore speak authoritatively on the scriptures based on their personal experience. A number have practiced for many years, secluded in caves or forests, and are well versed both in *samatha* and Vipassana.

In our understanding, the key difference is that *sati* is attention moment by moment, while *samadhi* is the level of concentration at each moment. It's one thing to concentrate, and quite another to detect and be attentive to the subtlest changes which occur in the passage from one moment of consciousness to the next. Of course, concentration (*samadhi*) is necessary to experience things as they are, but the Buddha's great innovation is that

Integral Vipassana

mental stability (*Samadhi*) requires more than just concentration. The use of the same word for an element of and for the whole system of attention, as well as the influence of an Indo-Tibetan Buddhism biased towards *samatha*, has led to equivocation.

> **Ceasing mental activities may lead to states of trance or ecstasy, but that these do not correspond to existential reality.**

Concentration is a part of the *Samadhi* group of the "Noble Eightfold Path." The Buddha's teaching is summarized in the Four Noble Truths: I experience dissatisfaction; this originates from attachment; there is a method to overcome this attachment; and that method is known as the Noble Eightfold Path—or simply "the Path." This Noble Eightfold Path comprises eight qualities: right speech, right conduct and livelihood, right resolve/right view, right concentration (*samadhi*), right mindfulness (*sati*), and right effort (*vayama*). The first three are called *sila* (and correspond to the ethical part of the method), the next two are known as *paññā* (and correspond to the philosophical aspect), and the last three are *Samadhi* (and correspond to the psychological component, which is developed through meditation).

The breakthrough in this understanding by the Buddha is that *concentration does not lead to liberation*. In proposing true *Samadhi* as "mental stability" or "mental health," he is saying that ceasing mental activities may lead to states of trance or ecstasy, but that these do not correspond to existential reality. The human organism is in dynamic interaction with everything else, and therefore mental and physical activities are its relative reality. "Awakening" is not to stop life but rather to realize that it is a relative reality and to disappear into it. Ceasing to exist as a separate entity from that reality is what we term entering into absolute reality. The method itself warns of attachment or stagnation in the *jhanas*—understood as being states of absorption (especially in individualistic and narcissistic societies such as ours)—and underlines the need for immersion in life as it is.

The Satipatthāna Sutta

The content of this book is built around a modern interpretation of the *Satipatthāna Sutta*, the section of Buddhism's Pali Canon, or *Tipitaka*, that describes in detail how to carry out the analysis of lived experience by paying attention to its components. This commentary aims to bridge the temporal, cultural, and epistemological differences that may make understanding it difficult for a contemporary mentality.

Here we reveal the contents of the *Sutta*, expanding on and explaining this ancient oral tradition in more modern terms that include the knowledge developed in Western psychology through the exhaustive analysis of physiology and neurology. The Western meditator has learned about the functioning of the human body, and this can be useful to contextualize the work of intuitive introspection or insight that characterizes meditative activity. For example, when the *Sutta* asks one to be attentive to posture and the movement of the body, the western meditator may understand that this is a reference to proprioception—that is to say, the system that deals with moving the body in space efficiently, and the balance and level of musculoskeletal tension at each moment.

The Pali Canon is divided into three parts (the three baskets): the speeches (*Sutta Pitaka*), monastic rules (*Vinaya Pitaka*), and the additional teachings (*Abhidhamma Pitaka*).

According to experts, there are strong parallels between some fundamental texts that have been called "early Buddhism." These coincidences are believed to be prior to the first schism between different schools, a schism that began some hundred years after the Buddha's death. The documents that make up the basket of discourses (and include those on monastic discipline found in Chinese, as well as some partial texts in Sanskrit and Tibetan) are all virtually identical to those of the Pali Canon. Some authors refer to this period as "early Buddhism," and these documents constitute the common basis of all subsequent schools. Although these translations date back to the fifth and sixth centuries, around a thousand years after the death of the Buddha, some of their parts are of the same age as the Pali Canon and corroborate it.

The *Pitaka Sutta* consists of five *nikayas*, or collections of sermons delivered by the Buddha. These are the ones that interest us in this work:

- *Digha Nikaya*, an anthology of thirty-four of the longest speeches focused on the spiritual formation of monks and nuns, the duties of the laity, and various other aspects of religious life of India in the fifth century BCE. It also contains a description of the qualities of the Buddha (*Sampasadaniya*) and the last days of his life (*Mahaparinibbana*).
- *Majjhima Nikaya*, an anthology of 152 speeches of medium length, including an extensive collection of stories about the Buddha, his struggle to achieve enlightenment, his first sermons, as well as some of the basic doctrines.
- *Samyutta Nikaya*, a collection of five series of *suttas*, divided into themes according to their content, such as the Noble Eightfold Path and the nature of human personality.
- *Anguttara Nikaya*, which has eleven sections of *suttas*, most of which are included in the other *nikayas*.
- *Khuddaka-Nikaya*, a collection of minor works that includes such popular texts as the *Dhammapada*, an anthology of poems by the Buddha; the *Udana*, a collection of some of the Buddha's maxims; the *Sutta-Nipata*, a collection of verses which includes some legends about the Buddha's life; and the *Jatakas*, stories about the Buddha's "past lives" to illustrate how *kamma* (past action) has consequences.

In general, the differences between the different versions of the *Nikayas* are not based on doctrinal or sectarian discrepancies between the different schools; instead, they can be considered to be the texts closest to what the Buddha actually taught. Other extremely important texts that will help one understand early Buddhism are the *Agamas*, translated out of Sanskrit or some other Prakrit language into Chinese.

We find versions of the *Satipatthāna Sutta* in the *Majjhima Nikaya*, as well as in the *Digha Nikaya* and the *Samyutta Nikaya*, which only mentions the formula or initial paragraph (*Satipatthāna Samyutta*) about the four registers or areas of experience. *Satipatthāna* is usually translated in two different ways: traditionally, as "foundations of attention," although more recently, experts have attributed a different root that is now translated as "to be present" or "to accompany." The complete resulting translation is now commonly accepted to be "the four areas of experience which must be accompanied by conscious attention" or "in which conscious attention must be present."

The versions of *Majjhima Nikaya* and *Digha Nikaya* are identical, except for the addition to the end of the "Four Noble Truths." Apparently, this addition corresponds to a commentary appended to the Canon when the *Abhidhamma* was emerging, which, as we have seen, does not belong to the contents of so-called "early Buddhism," but rather is appreciably later.

The version of *Digha Nikaya* is known as *Mahasatipattana Sutta* ("maha" is a prefix meaning "the most important"). The translation would be, "the most important discourse on the four areas of experience where conscious attention must be present." The *Digha* version is the most venerated in those countries of the Theravada tradition and is also the most attractive for scholars and sages of the *Dhamma*.

Nevertheless, this does not mean that it is necessarily the most primary or original form. We have chosen the versions of the Pali Canon which follow the Theravada tradition, but there are other schools' versions that also have a claim for authenticity.

Three Complete Versions, and More

There are at least three complete versions of the *Sutta*—the Pali version, which we will use, and two in Chinese. One of the Chinese versions is attributed to the monk Sanghadeva, who translated it from Sanskrit in 389 CE, and would seem to belong to the *Sarvastivada* school. The other would appear to have been translated directly from Prakrit and not from Sanskrit. It is considered a text of the *Mahasanghika* school, the first schism of the ancient *Sthavira*.

The Theravada School of Sri Lanka and Southeast Asia has been exclusively associated with the *Sthaviras*, since the Pali word *thera* is equivalent to Sanskrit *sthavira*. However, this is not the case. In Ashoka's time, the *Sthavira* sect was divided into *Sammitīya Pudgalavada*, *Sarvāstivāda*, and *Vibhajyavāda* schools. The *Vibhajyavāda* school is believed to have been subdivided into other schools, including the *Mahīsāsaka* school that is considered to be the ancestor of the Theravada school. There is no historical evidence that the Theravada school arose until two centuries after the great schism that occurred in the Third Council.

A fourth and incomplete version appears in the *Prajnaparamita Sutras*, a corpus of foundational texts of the *Mahayana* tradition.

The discrepancies are various. Some people believe the original version did not include the practices related to the observation of the body, nor those associated with the observation of *dhammas*. While some suggest that the text refers to individual experience, others consider it to be about knowledge of the mind in general. For instance, when talking about the process of bodily decomposition, obviously it cannot be referring to our own body, whereas when it talks of observing breath, it seems highly unlikely that it is referring to our observation of another person. The commentaries and subtleties as to what is original teaching and what was later added by the oral reciters are endless speculations that exceed the practical objectives of this presentation.

A Guide for Insightful Meditation

We consider the *Satipatthāna* to be a personal guide to the path of insight meditation—the largest contribution that the Buddha's *Dhamma* made to meditation. Existential dissatisfaction, the "First Noble Truth," cannot be overcome by *samatha* meditation or the tranquility meditation that the Buddha learned from his teachers. *Samatha* meditation, despite leading to extremely deep and serene states of consciousness, did not allow him to achieve the wisdom needed to live in this world without dissatisfaction. Of course, concentration (*samadhi*) is a fundamental part of the Buddha's method, but if dynamic attention or conscious attention (*sati*) is not developed at the same time, with an adequate level of attentional activation (*vayama*), there can be no understanding of the origin of dissatisfaction, the

"Second Noble Truth," and therefore, its resolution or cessation, the "Third Noble Truth."

The "Fourth Noble Truth" of the *Dhamma*, the Noble Eightfold Path, includes *samadhi* as well as *sati* and *vayama*.

If we do not heed what has been transmitted to us—if all eight elements of the Path are not developed—then we will not achieve release from dissatisfaction. We consider all this information to be necessary to confront a text with such ambiguous characteristics. But we must also remember what is in the *Kalama Sutta*. In this *Sutta*, the Buddha passes by the village of Kesaputta, and its inhabitants, the Kalamas, request his advice: "Many gurus pass through the village with their own teachings and criticizing those of others! Which should we follow?" The Buddha responded as follows:

> *Do not go upon what has been acquired by repeated hearing; nor upon tradition; nor upon rumor; nor upon what is in a scripture; nor upon surmise; nor upon an axiom; nor upon specious reasoning; nor upon a bias towards a notion that has been pondered over; nor upon another's seeming ability; nor upon the consideration, "The monk is our teacher." Kalamas, when you yourselves know: "These things are good; these things are not blamable; these things are praised by the wise; undertaken and observed, these things lead to benefit and happiness," enter on and abide in them.*

In this regard, the interpretation that we propose in these pages is limited to our meditative experience, our training in the tradition of the Buddha, and our personal perspective of his teaching, which is not religious but rather *psychological and transpersonal*. As noted in the Preface, we approach this interpretation especially with respect to the work of American philosopher and author Ken Wilber, who developed integral theory as a synthesis of all human knowledge and experience. We are also indebted to later developments in cognitive neuroscience and affective neuroscience.

Our intention is that this approach prove useful for people who undertake meditation as a form of personality advancement and also as a type of self-transcendence, understanding the latter is the key to overcoming existential dissatisfaction.

How To Read This Book

Integral Vipassana views *sati* (mindfulness)—which we call "conscious attention"—as the activity of the organism (mind-body) that leads directly to freedom from existential dissatisfaction. In other words, mindfulness will lead us to wisdom, the objective of the Buddha's method.

From the point of view of the Buddha's *Dhamma*, the only thing that exists is first-person experience. Behavior, as well as the external world, is included in this experience and not vice versa. Science is based on the premise that things (objects that have a spatiotemporal location) are all that exist, and that they interact according to the laws of nature. Its starting point is that there is a reality independent from the observer and therefore that there is such a concept as objective knowledge. The *Dhamma*, however, holds that subject and object are mutually constructed, thereby giving rise to a relative and interdependent reality. This constructive (enactive) activity is precisely what conscious attention discovers, so revealing the attraction, rejection, excitation, and lethargy that produce dissatisfaction.

Clearly it is impossible to comprehensively represent these two distinct worldviews—that of the Buddha and of Western science, each set down in different languages and including different activities, levels, states and types —in a mere diagram. However, Figure 3 expresses the purpose of this book, which is none other than to interconnect two approaches to something as dynamic and complex as human experience. It is not intended to be complete or the truth but rather to help you imagine and reflect upon the meditative experience.

Introduction

	INTEGRAL VIPASSANA			
SATI	GROWING		AWAKENING	WISDOM
	Content of experience		Flow of experience	
PAÑÑA	3. COGNITIONS Attention, Motivation, Perception *Mental consciousness* *Autobiographical self* Cortical regions		4. STATES OF CONSCIOUSNESS INTENTION — VOLUNTARY / INVOLUNTARY Conscious regulation	ANATTA IMPERSONALITY Manas – Viññana
SAMADHI	2. FEELINGS Learning and memory *Emotional consciousness* *Nucleur affective ego* Basal ganglia and upper limbic region		ORIENTATION — ATTRACTION / REJECTION Learnt control	DUKHA INSATISFACTION Vedana – Manas
SILA				
VAYAMA	1. SENSATIONS Homeostasis, Interoceptive, Sensory *Bodily consciousness* *Proto-self* Subcortical regions		ALERTNESS — EXCITATION / LETHARGY	ANICCA IMPERMANENCE Nama – Rupa
NOBLE EIGHTFOLD PATH	PSYCHOLOGICAL PROCESSES	INCLUDE AND TRASCEND	ATTENTION NETWORKS SELF-REGULATING SYSTEMS	CHARACTERISTICS OF EXISTENCE
	FOUR FOUNDATIONS OF MINDFULNESS			

Figure 3: A schema of Integral Vipassana that integrates psychological maturation and spiritual awakening.

The Noble Eightfold Path is divided into three sections: *Sila* (ethics), *Samadhi* (psychology), and *Pañña* (philosophy). However the psychological block is composed of: *vayama* (organismic activation), *samadhi* (attentional focus), *sati* (constant conscious attention) and is worked on through meditation. Mental stability (*Samadhi*) depends on ethical calm (*Sila*) and harmonious vision (*Pañña*).

In the center of the diagram, you will see the interpretation of the "four foundations of attention," couched in terms of contemporary knowledge, which we further develop in the commentary. The first three evolve in a nested structure, "bottom-up," as it is termed nowadays. In the fourth, the activity of the three attention networks regulates the ever-changing flow of states of consciousness (top-down).

The book is divided into two main parts. The first incorporates this Introduction and an introductory major chapter, "The Development of Conscious Awareness." In that chapter we discuss the first three paragraphs of the *Sutta* and the "refrain" characteristic of oral traditions. These address the necessary attitude one must adopt to undertake contemplation, as well as the disposition needed during formal meditation practice.

The book's second major part encompasses four chapters devoted to the four foundations of attention:
- Contemplation of Somatic Activities
- Contemplation of the Activities of Feeling
- Contemplation of the Activities of Knowing
- Contemplation of the Phenomena of Experience

The path of *sati* integrates contemplation of the four types of experience: somatic, affective, and cognitive experiences, and the *flow* of experience—the dynamic process of the other three exactly as we experience it moment by moment.

Chapter Structure: Three Texts

Each chapter starts with a summary that introduces the reader to its essentials. Following that is the corresponding part of the *Sutta*. Finally, it provides commentary on each of the four foundations of attention. So, there are three texts in play—the original, the commentary, and the abstract.

Using this approach, you can focus your attention on a single component of somatic experience (such as when you pay attention to breathing), on affective experience (for example, when you practice compassion meditation), or on cognitive experience (such as when you recite a mantra). This is how you learn to discriminate between sensations, feelings, and cognitions. The result is that you comprehend the true composition of experience, thereby eradicating the beliefs, prejudices, and distortions that underlie its interpretation.

Attention can open you up to the flow of experience as it occurs moment by moment, thereby making you aware of the shifting nature of consciousness. The result is that you learn the causal relationships responsible for these changes. This reveals the imbalances, habits, and regularities of alertness, orientation, and intention, the three attention networks that are the regulatory systems of organismic activity (e.g. when we do Vipassana). This revelation destroys the causal links that lead to unhealthy states of consciousness, which in turn leads to the self-regulation of the experience and the re-establishment of its natural flow.

When you practice focusing your attention on the first three attention networks, you are carrying out a *constructive* activity because a state of consciousness is being generated voluntarily. When you practice opening up to the flow of experience, you are engaging in a *deconstructive* activity because you understand that these states of consciousness are the result of causes and conditions, many of which do not depend on your will but rather are premises of very existence.

The meditator may try to voluntarily direct attention toward a physical sensation or mental activity, but what really happens is that the four foundations are continually being turned on and off. The process escapes the conscious intentions of the subject, and precisely because of this, the meditator discovers that subject and object are not distinct and independent entities, but rather dependent on causes and conditions that fluctuate moment by moment.

The balanced activity of the three attention networks, when controlled by executive attention or conscious attention (*sati*), reveals the subject-object relationships—what we today call "third person knowledge of first-person experience." The subject begins to discover the causal relationships with its physical, affective, and cognitive objects. Through contemplating the flow of experience, spiritual awakening occurs—that is to say, the subject-object duality is resolved.

Direct experience (rather than interpreted or "first-person experience") starts to harmonize and give rise to unitary states of consciousness that include and transcend the characteristics of existence (impermanence, dissatisfaction, impersonality), resulting in what is traditionally called wisdom.

THE DEVELOPMENT OF CONSCIOUS AWARENESS

In this chapter we introduce a series of elements that we consider to be necessary before addressing the four foundations of attention one by one. We will begin by exploring what dissatisfaction is for the Buddha. Later, we explain that the Buddha's method to overcome it requires the practice of a particular type of meditation that includes the development of conscious attention, or *sati*.

Before introducing the three introductory paragraphs of the *Sutta*, we will describe for the first time the four foundations and then present the version of the *Sutta* that we have chosen.

We will explain what the motivation is behind our interpretation of the Buddha's discourse, as well as the limits of our perspective.

In order to clarify that meditation is not about accumulating knowledge but rather about understanding the workings of the mind, we investigate the difference between "first-person experience," which is the only reality for the Buddha, and "third-person experience," which is the interpretation or explanation of "first-person experience." The "third-person experience" is what the Western mindset considers knowledge, but it is not the kind of knowledge that develops when meditating.

We then present what, in our opinion, is one of the fundamental contributions of the book: Buddha's proposition that attention is the fundamental tool for meditation. We explore the relationship between what Western psychology today knows about attention and the place that attention occupies in the Buddha's method. We proceed to analyze the first three paragraphs, differentiating between "thinking slowly" and "thinking fast," as expounded by Daniel Kahneman.

We complete the analysis with two significant clarifications—the first about one of the most discussed formulations amongst interpreters of the *Sutta*, and the second about the two-way flow of information in the human organism ("bottom-up" and "top-down"). Both are contributions of contemporary psychology, which, if not well understood, may confuse the meditator and impede progress.

Finally, we analyze the refrain, as we view its three characteristics of existence to be the key to Vipassana meditation.

The Four Foundations of Attention

The *Satipatthāna Sutta* is structured into four areas of experience—or four domains of the organism's activity—that must be accompanied by conscious attention (*sati*). The first three correspond to the three areas where consciousness operates—sensory awareness, affective awareness, and cognitive awareness. These are differentiable domains, even if they do appear undifferentiated due to the speed at which they metamorphose and interweave. These are the domains that we can talk about: We all have a body, we all feel, and we all know. Biological and neuroscientific theories are based on these—they are the third-person knowledge of first-person experience.

On the other hand, the fourth domain is the flow of mental phenomena or lived experience—our private, moment-to-moment experience of reality. This phenomenological awareness is the first-person knowledge of the first-person experience.

Lived experience is the only information that we have. However, that information can be known from different perspectives. Science accomplishes this from a third-person position. The second perspective is accomplished when we put ourselves in the place of the other. When we talk about our experiences, we use the first person. Utilizing a private access that is limited to our own experience, we call this a "first-person knowledge of first-person experience." To nurture *sati* implies different degrees of attentional control, different levels in the relationships between knowing and knowledge, and different procedures. The *Sutta* is a journey through how human consciousness has been constructed moment by moment, interleaving these four domains into the experience in progress.

We have chosen the translation of *Nyanasatta Thera* as it is the closest to our understanding of the text.[1] Nevertheless, as will be seen later, we do not agree with some of the translator's decisions, and we will therefore offer alternative translations as part of the commentary.

Satipatthāna Sutta: The Four Foundations of Mindfulness

Thus have I heard. At one time the Blessed One was living among the Kurus, at Kammasadamma, a market town of the Kuru people. There the Blessed One addressed the bhikkhu thus: "Monks," and they replied to him, "Venerable Sir." The Blessed One spoke as follows:

This is the only way, monks, for the purification of beings, for the overcoming of sorrow and lamentation, for the destruction of suffering and grief, for reaching the right path, for the attainment of Nibbana, namely, the four foundations of mindfulness. What are the four?

Herein (in this teaching) a monk lives contemplating the body in the body, ardent, clearly comprehending and mindful, having overcome, in this world, covetousness and grief; he lives contemplating feelings in feelings, ardent, clearly comprehending and mindful, having overcome, in this world, covetousness and grief; he lives contemplating consciousness in consciousness, ardent, clearly comprehending and mindful, having overcome, in this world, covetousness and

---

1 "Satipatthāna Sutta: The Foundations of Mindfulness" (MN 10) Translated from the Pali by Nyanasatta Thera, 1994. https://www.accesstoinsight.org/tipitaka/mn/mn.010.nysa.html

grief; he lives contemplating mental objects in mental objects, ardent, clearly comprehending and mindful, having overcome, in this world, covetousness and grief.

Intention

Our analysis of this is intended to make this form of meditation, based on conscious attention, comprehensible and applicable for people today. Human knowledge has evolved over the intervening 2,500 years and human language has adapted itself to this new knowledge. Our way of life has been transformed and, with it, human experience. Despite there being much in common, the psyche has adapted to profound changes. Today we are subjected to a tremendous amount of stimuli that bombard us through media that simply did not exist in Buddha's time. We live frenetically when compared to the rural life back then, and this has transformed our mental activity. Our cultural forms are radically different from those of that bygone culture, and modern societies involve many codes and norms that did not exist then.

> **Today we are subjected to a tremendous amount of stimuli that that simply did not exist in Buddha's time.**

We are unlikely to find valid answers for our existential circumstances by digging into the etymology of words from an extremely ancient language that has been transmitted, interpreted, and translated at different historical moments by people from very diverse cultural backgrounds. Accordingly, we do not believe that there is one single interpretation of the *Sutta*, but rather successive attempts to make the knowledge accumulated in the text comprehensible to the mentality of each era. In that sense, we do not feel indebted to any lineage, nor do we feel any obligation to be faithful to any particular doctrine. While we do this exercise from a position of intellectual freedom, we remain confined nevertheless by the limits of what we have learned from our meditative practice, from the teachings we have received, and from our development as human beings.

Attention

In cognitive terms, the Buddha's discovery is that attention is the doorway to knowledge and the access to our awareness.

Attention is a basic psychological process which, even today, we still do not how to fully explain. What Buddha understood is that *samadhi*, as it was practiced in his time, was limited to concentration and did not lead to liberation. His method of meditation sets in motion a system of attention where concentration is only a part.

Concentration is the ability to keep attention focused on an object, or on the task being performed. However, attention involves a lot more tasks that control and manage mental processes, such as sorting the information received through the senses, dealing with distraction, carrying out two tasks simultaneously, detecting errors, paying attention to language, and developing working memory (working with/analyzing data), task changing, etc. In addition, the result of the attention process is compared in the working memory with all previously acquired information—all the memories, judgments, beliefs, associations, reaction patterns, and habits. That allows one to be able to choose the perceptual hypothesis that best fits the information provided by attention and finally, create perception.

In short, Buddha realized that *samadhi* as concentration did not allow the process of perception-building to become conscious, and it is precisely this perception we have of reality—our erroneous vision—that is the root of dissatisfaction. A correct level of concentration together with a correct amount of effort are basic requirements for conscious attention to be able to access the mind's own activities and perform self-transcendence.

Instead of focusing attention on an object, it is advisable to work on developing a more wide-open attention that may simply be present amidst the continuous flux of phenomena. In other words, conscious attention (*sati*).

Nevertheless, for attention to be harmonious, it must be well-focused—i.e., one has to ensure that all attentional resources are directed at the current phenomenon (*samadhi*).

Attention also requires a precise level of activation (*vayama*). The greater the activation, the faster the detection of the stimulus. On the other hand, this increased activation can also lead to lower precision and more anticipatory responses and errors.

In short, every moment has its *sati*, its *samadhi*, and its *vayama*. Buddha's discovery of this is in line with most attention theories developed by contemporary psychology and neuroscience. They all consider attention to be a system with, at minimum, three basic functions or neurological networks: control, selection, and alertness. Nevertheless, Buddha's method does not require scientific knowledge nor the reduction of experience to physiological explanations. Merely analyzing lived experience should be enough to lead to liberation from existential dissatisfaction.

The Buddha's method for this liberation consists of three major sections: ethics (*sila*), beliefs and intentions (*paññā*), and psychology (*Samadhi*). The psychological aspect (*Samadhi*) is a system for paying attention to each moment of the lived experience and is comprised of three elements: selection (*samadhi*), alertness (*vayama*), and control (*sati*). It is precisely this attentional system that is cultivated in meditation.

The *Samadhi* in Buddha's *Dhamma* is not concentration or calmness, but rather a system of conscious attention that can be honed until the practitioner can experience and understand how the human mind works (see Figure 4), an understanding that will ultimately reveal the origin of dissatisfaction.

Approach: The First Three Paragraphs

"Thus have I heard" is the way in which all the discourses (*suttas*) in the Pali Canon begin. As noted in the introduction, after Buddha's death these discourses were handed down orally. In the first council, Ananda, who had accompanied and looked after the Buddha and who, it is said, had a privileged memory, was in charge of reciting the speeches. So, this first sentence "Thus have I heard," is what Ananda says before starting the story.

Next, we normally hear where, or with whom, the Buddha was on that occasion, which is extremely helpful for authenticating the texts, for

The Development of Conscious Awareness

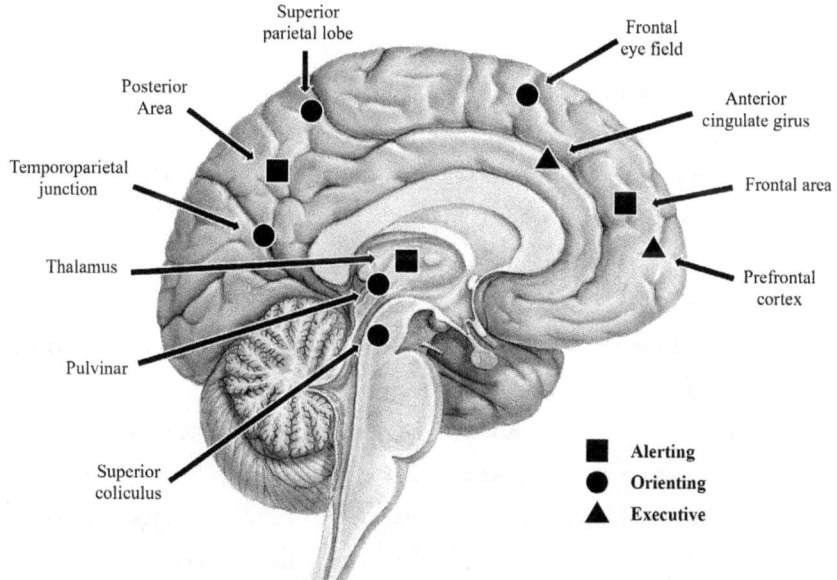

Network	Function	Samadhi
Alerting Network	Excitation – Lethargy. Organism activation level.	vayama
Orienting Network	Attraction – Rejection. Orient, disengage, reorient, filter, fix, and focus.	samadhi
Executive Network	Sustained attention, attentional conflict resolution, two-task coordinated performance, error detection, attention to language, working memory, and decision making.	sati

Figure 4: The three attention networks and their relation to the Dhamma.

following the Buddha's path in his teaching, or for understanding how he adapted his words to his listeners.

The first sentence of the second paragraph, "Monks, this is the path of one direction," has been translated in several ways: "only path," "direct path," "one-way path." Whatever it may mean, it refers to the path of *sati*, not to that of *samadhi*. The sentences that follow speak of the relevant steps on the path to be undertaken: purification, "devictimization," mental health, wisdom, and liberation. The passage concludes with a phrase that is also open to interpretation. Here we understand "foundations of attention" as being the whole range of the organism's activities in which conscious attention (*sati*) must be present. We must remember that when we speak of organisms, we refer to "mind/body" as a functional unit.

The third paragraph lays out the four areas of experience, as well as how they should be contemplated. It establishes the attitude with which we approach meditation. *Sati*, or conscious attention, is the key to that attitude (*Satipatthāna*). Initially, there is a presence or an absence of *sati*—in other words, there is *conscious attention* or there is *conditioned attention* (automatic pilot). We observe the process of the experience step by step, or we fall back into the usual rapid, automatic way of experiencing things that we use in daily life. We experience every moment of reality either as if for the first time, or as a routine reality.

These days we think that the organism has developed two forms of processing incoming information. One is conscious and depends on attention—it is a controlled process, explicit, and requires effort. The other is automatic—implicit, effortless, and non-attentional. Automatic or *unconscious processing* is said to function "in parallel," handling many different types of data at high speed, but *conscious* or *attentional processing* works "in series," step by step, following an order, one activity at a time.

When an activity stops being novel, it loses priority access to consciousness. The repetition reinforces the connections between the stimuli, the objectives, and the responses, so that the activity can be carried out completely effortlessly.

These two different ways of operating have to do with the fact that attention has a limited capacity and so creates a system of automated routines, thereby increasing the number of operations that we can carry out without having to think about them. This non-conscious activity is the product of conscious training, adopted by the mind to save resources and energy. Conscious activities require more effort and expend more energy than reactive activities.

You can perform several simultaneous tasks just as long as the resources you use are different, occupy different planes, or depend on different sensory channels. You can read while listening to music if the latter is kept in the background, but if you listen to music as a foreground you cannot read. You can drive and listen to music at the same time, but reading and watching TV at the same time is almost impossible. This all depends, as we have said, on the ability we have to carry out each task. The better you know how to do something, the easier it becomes and the less attention you have to dedicate to it, as you are able to delegate the control of its execution to the automatic processing system, which works in parallel. That frees up conscious resources to perform other tasks.

That these two ways of processing exist explains just how quickly we digest information, as well as how we can so rapidly differentiate information that is uncategorized or degraded, distorted, clipped, or overlapping. This also explains how we can keep on processing even when our mind is not at its best because it is sleepy, fatigued, or injured. It allows us to deal with multiple or simultaneous demands and lets us complete conceptual and perceptive patterns without necessarily having all the information. The system is capable of self-organization—in other words, it can adapt to the demands of the environment without needing a controller to supervise the work, and without the need for anybody to notice, or start, the automated operations.

> **Human beings build their reality moment by moment from sensory stimuli and their mental representations.**

When using fast automatic processing, data self-relate via multiple connections and then form networks. The networks are created by the strength of connection and are activated or inhibited depending on this force. There are no representations, classified and memorized, nor formal rules to relate them. It is the degree of activation or inhibition propagating around the network that generates a pattern. This pattern becomes a perceptive hypothesis, and it triggers when information enters the system that is similar to that which initiated it, even if we do not have all the necessary information. The units of a network are activated mutually, thereby increasing the strength of the connection—this is how learning occurs.

Human beings build their reality moment by moment from sensory stimuli and their mental representations. These are processed unconsciously through learned patterns, thereby giving structure and meaning to what is received partially and chaotically from the different sensory channels. The incoming information is an overwhelming torrent of unconnected and elementary data that are continuously modified and then displaced by the data that follow. Each of the channels—including five physical senses plus that of the intellect—transmits physicochemical signals whose modifications are received by neurons and specialized neural networks that activate the aforementioned accumulated perceptual hypotheses. These are possibilities of information interpretation based on previous experiences, contributing an adaptive sense to the incoming information.

In all these activities there is a minimum part that is conscious. This saves considerable energy and effort when compared to conscious, step-by-step processing. So perception is subject to a complex process of elaboration whose result has little to do with what exists in the external world. Perception is an interpretation useful for the survival of the organism or social adaptation. However it is not "reality" nor its faithful representation.

The Buddha faced the challenge of discovering how the human mind works without the knowledge we possess today in physiology or neuroscience. His only tool was the ability of the human mind to access its own experiential world. Therefore, the language he uses must necessarily be symbolic, ambiguous, and sometimes cryptic. The four areas of application of *sati* do not adapt well to our way of thinking, nor to our everyday language, which is why they have been the object of interpretation and commentary in every historical epoch.

To introduce the first three scopes of inquiry, the *Sutta* says something that is omitted in some translations and that we intend to interpret slightly differently from the translation we have chosen. Instead of "the monk lives contemplating the body in the body," we have chosen to translate this passage as "the monk sees the body *as* a body" ("*bhikkhu kaye kayanupassi*").

Sensation vs. Feeling

Before proceeding we must address a conceptual and terminological problem that affects all subsequent interpretation. In our analysis of the *Sutta* we refer to what is meant by "body," "sensations," and "mind." As we have noted, the Buddha undertook the investigation of suffering with just the one tool: attention to his own experience. He tried to understand exactly what in this experience produces suffering, and also whether an experience free of suffering is possible.

Methodologically, the *Sutta* divides experience into three classifications. When dealing with the body, it refers to bodily or *somatic* experience. When referring to the sensations, it references the experience of *feeling*. Discussions of the mind refer to the experience of *knowing*.

According to this method, all contact is evaluated or felt, and with this information the object is "known." Through Vipassana we learn to *react consciously to what is felt*. To understand how attachment comes about, we need to clarify what in the *Sutta* is called contact, evaluation, and reaction.

In natural language, "feeling" is applied to sensations, perceptions, emotions, intuitions, opinions, or judgments ("I say what I feel"). It is applied to pleasure or pain, hunger or cold, love or hatred, fatigue or illness. Some of these are somatic activities, while others are cognitive.

> **We call all incoming physical sensory data "sensation" and all immediate cognitive assessment "feeling."**

At this point we are forced to make a terminological choice—more or less in accordance with customary uses of popular or scientific language—that does not adhere to the terms used in the *Sutta* translation we have chosen. We call all incoming physical sensory data "sensation" and all immediate cognitive assessment "feeling." Both sensations and feelings belong to the general activity of consciousness (even if they may not be conscious). You experience a sensation, and you feel a feeling.

Somatic activity is to make contact, and feeling activity is to evaluate the contact as pleasant, unpleasant, or neutral. Feeling is a form of cognition. We suffer because we react by clinging to pleasant feelings and rejecting unpleasant ones. We find pleasure (or we suffer) precisely because we like (or dislike) what we feel.

The activity of feeling appears in any somatic activity, and any somatic activity is valued affectively. Consequently, they are not part of different realities, but rather two aspects of the same reality. Feeling is part of the activity of knowing, or cognition, whose most immediate experience is perception. The mind, which includes cognition or the activity of knowing, is built from the basic matrix of feeling—pleasant, unpleasant, neutral—and feeds off somatic activity or sensation.

So, we have a three-level nested structure. The somatic level is included in the affective, and the affective, in turn, in the cognitive. The somatic level is more basic than the affective level, which is more basic than the cognitive level. This means that without the somatic level there can be no affective—or, later, cognitive—levels. Again, *this structure does not have to mold itself to scientific knowledge*, given that the method consists of contemplation of experience in the first person. This is precisely what makes it a universal method—anyone and everyone has direct access to their own experience.

To sum up, when in the translation of the *Sutta* there is a reference to "contemplation of the body," we interpret this as "contemplation of somatic activity" and refer to it as sensation. Where "contemplation of sensations" is translated, we prefer to speak of "contemplation of the activities of feeling" and we call it feeling. And where "contemplation of the consciousness" is translated, we speak of "contemplation of the activities of knowing" and we call it cognition.

So, returning to the *Sutta*, the propositions "attends to somatic activity as a somatic activity," "the activity of feeling as an activity of feeling," "the activity of knowing as an activity of knowing" make sense if we take into account that the Buddha's method contains its own structure of attention. What this perceptive man probably realized is that each of the three registers (somatic, affective, and cognitive) is experienced via its

> **This is not about interpreting or reducing feelings to mere physical sensations, but about really feeling the feelings.**

very own attentional network. Hence, sensory awareness is experienced through a network that heeds the activation level of the physical organism, affective awareness through a network that attends to affective preferences, and cognitive awareness through a network that attends to cognitive and executive activities. Each of the three registers has its own monitoring system, which must be used and developed in meditation.

This is not about feeling or thinking about the body, but about *experiencing* the body in its materiality and biological order. In the same way, this is not about interpreting or reducing feelings to mere physical sensations, but about really *feeling* the feelings. Feelings cause the organism to approach or distance itself from the object and activate a behavior (physical or mental) of retention or avoidance. Desire and the response to desire is the object of this register.

Neither is it a question of feeling or physically experiencing cognitive activities, but of *becoming aware of them*. It's not about wanting to have (or not have) this or the other thought, or of experiencing the activities of the organism which underlie the thought. *It's about what we know* and the exact activities that lead to this knowing. In short, the point is to observe each register with the system developed for that specific function.

Obviously, the Buddha did not know of the existence of specialized attentional networks, but the contemplation of the construction of human consciousness led him to realize that it was imperative to attend to each of the domains individually so as to be able to uncover the causal order in which they interrelate.

In modern terminology, we would be talking about the attention systems processing information "top-down." Attention is a cognitive process that deals with incoming information. Cognitive processes can be managed intentionally, depending on expectations, task requirements, and/or planned outcomes—in other words, on affective preferences. The cognitive systems, such as attention, respond to incoming "bottom-up" processes, which are the primary sensations and feelings that we share with other species. Therefore, there are incoming primary feelings and also secondary feelings that moderate the former. These secondary feelings include the three attentional systems that let in the information being processed by the cognitive systems, such as motivation, memory, perception, thought, or language.

It is interesting to note that affective life goes right through human beings. There is incoming affective information and respondent affective information, which is why we confuse pure physical sensations with their affective evaluations. One can experience incoming affective sensations and outgoing affective reactions without the need for an "I," though this does not exclude acting consciously.

The human organism is subject to conditions that impact the senses, as well as to vital impulses and cognitive activities, inescapable for proper functioning. It has some systems that receive information and others that elaborate it to produce an adaptive response. Some we call "bottom-up" and the others "top-down."

Using the top-down processes, you can voluntarily move your hand, choose to not react to an unpleasant smell, or to stop thinking about something, but there is bottom-up information you cannot avoid. You cannot stop your skin from getting scraped if you fall over; you cannot stop yourself from having a survival instinct (although it can be suspended by a "top-down" decision); and you cannot stop yourself from constructing mental representations (although they can be stopped by higher-level executive functions).

The Dhammas

The result of all this activity is the fourth foundation of attention, the *dhammas*. These are the mental phenomena that constitute the phenomenological experience. They are the product of primary activities (somatic, affective, and cognitive), and of their management by the attentional networks and the rest of the executive activities. Nevertheless, the primary activities—such as the physiological and procedural, the primary affective programs, or the basic psychological processes—work unconsciously. Most of these activities are carried out by the attentional systems, while the other top-down activities are automated and function as judgments, preferences, and unconscious habits.

In fact, what appears in the phenomenological experience is a minimal part of what the organism is doing continuously. We are only aware of an infinitesimally small part of the activity of the mind/body, but the strange thing is that with this minute part we are able to know ourselves and the world.

The Vipassana Perspective

It seems that the Buddha was intimately aware of this process in which we ignore and misunderstand the working of the mind and how it constructs the phenomenological experience. Indeed, he named it "ignorance." To deal with this situation, he developed Vipassana meditation, which allows the meditator to penetrate the intricate world of the mind and turn ignorance into wisdom. His form of meditation trained the attention system he had discovered to access the experienceable activities that occur in the human organism, thereby discovering their influence in existential dissatisfaction.

To put it metaphorically, the only way to do this is to pay attention, frame by frame, to the whole film—hence the importance of *sati*, conscious attention in every moment. To view each frame clearly, you have to focus well, which is the function of concentration or *samadhi*. Focusing and observing change are two activities that are almost contradictory. It seems that to focus well, you have to fix your attention, but if you fix your attention, you stop it from moving, which means you cannot see the process. If the object of attention is fixed, you learn to fix your attention, but if the objects change, then attention has to jump from one object to another. Conscious attention is awareness of attention—not just awareness of the object of attention—and therefore has to include an awareness of changes in attention as well as changes in the object.

You can focus on something fixed, but how do you focus on something that is constantly moving and changing? Trying to do both activities at the same time creates tension in the mind and consumes a lot of energy. As a tense or tired mind cannot do this work well, you have to find a way to make it more relaxing for the body and the mind. For this, you need an energy management system, which is *vayama*.

Using the entire system, you can begin to see the frames that are hidden by the speed of the process and penetrate into those areas of "top-down" processing that might be called *pre-conscious*. These are frames that were seen before but that have since disappeared from view: the conditioned affects (which belong to the second foundation of attention), and the cognitive dissonances that affect cognitive activities (typical of the third foundation of attention).

This third paragraph of the *Sutta* proposes that conscious attention must be present in these four registers of human experience, and to this end, meditators need to adopt a certain attitude.

As we have seen, conscious processing requires effort, and therefore meditation also requires enthusiasm, commitment, intensity, and perseverance (*atapi*). Furthermore, attention must be maintained while recognizing that there are different types of phenomena and activities (*sampajañña*) occurring one after another in a dynamic process that cannot be interrupted (*satima*). It must be impartial attention, in other words, without expectations or mundane preferences (*vineyya loke abhijjha domanassam*). This suspension of searching for affective reinforcements invokes a purification of intentionality. Together with the other qualities, it constitutes a meta-awareness attitude characteristic of Vipassana meditation.

The order in which the *Sutta* presents these four registers, or foundations, is important, although they cannot be understood simply as a series where the development of one is followed by the development of the other. The four foundations are active in the lived experience, and in meditation, we simultaneously advance the realization of their interaction. In other words, as soon as we begin to understand how the experience is produced, it begins to harmonize. We understand that unhealthy states produce unhealthy consequences, and they are replaced by healthy states that produce healthy consequences.

Refrain

The *Sutta* includes a refrain that is repeated after each paragraph. Given its continual repetition, we must understand it to be somewhat important. Translators, as interpreters, do not agree on its form or its meaning.

Our interpretation is that the refrain serves as a continual reminder of those three characteristics of all that exists: *dukkha* (dissatisfaction), *anatta* (non-self), and *anicca* (impermanence), bearing in mind that from the perspective of the Buddha's *Dhamma*, a thought or a feeling exists in the same way as a physical sensation. The three characteristics are uncovered thanks to *sati*, or conscious attention. Everything that exists is changing or impermanent, and therefore cannot be continuously satisfactory. In other words, it is unsatisfactory. If I cannot control even what refers to myself, for instance, I cannot make my body *not* change or age, nor can I feel only pleasant feelings and avoid unpleasant ones all the time. In the end, I cannot consider that "I" am a permanent and satisfactory entity.

When the *Sutta* says "live contemplating the body in the body," this statement becomes clearer and agrees with our new interpretation, which is for us to say, "live contemplating the body as a body," etc. Each thing is contemplated as it is, without mediation or mixing registers. The body, for example, is not contemplated as if it were a concept—that is to say, as a mental abstraction—nor as an object of desire composed of affective assessments. The body is neither pretty nor ugly, fat nor thin, "I like it" nor "I don't like it." The body, as it is experienced, is simply an amalgamation of physical sensations such as solidity, pressure, flexion, tightness, cold, heat, itching, tingling, etc. It is a direct experience of its materiality.

> **Experience is not the activity of the body or the brain, nor that of an agent that builds it. Rather, it is the result of prior causes and conditions.**

Integral Vipassana

In the case of feelings, we only register their condition of pleasant, unpleasant, or neutral. In the case of cognitions, we recognize the concepts, images, and thoughts that we apply to the feelings. Although they all have their physical or neuronal correlate, *sati* is directed toward the experience and neither reduces it to the underlying physiological processes nor identifies with it. In fact, *sati* limits itself to "contemplation"—in other words, to being present. Experience is not the activity of the body or the brain, nor that of an agent that builds it. Rather, it is the result of prior causes and conditions.

When the *Sutta* says that one has to contemplate "internally," "externally," or "both internally and externally," it is referring, precisely, to the limit—to the border that makes contemplation possible. To contemplate, there must be something that contemplates and something that is contemplated. We say that what is contemplated is *outside* and what is contemplating is *inside*.

So, for instance, contemplating the body as a body externally refers to an activity that is contemplating the contact points between the body as matter, and the matter that is not the body. Contemplating the body as a body internally is talking about the activity of contemplation as being directed towards the experience of that contact. The contact is observed, and the experience of the contact is observed. If one observes the contact, it will be seen that body matter and matter that is external to the body impact each other. But if the internal experience of the contact is contemplated, what you get is a physical sensation.

These two perspectives coexist, and we can place ourselves in one, in another, or in both. Seen this way, neither the surface of the body nor physical sensation are the activity of contemplation, but rather they are the two *perspectives* of contemplation.

While the contemplation activity is occurring, that which is being contemplated cannot identify with it—neither the body nor the somatic experience is the contemplation or the contemplator.

The same thing happens with feelings and the experience of feeling, or with knowledge and the experience of knowing. Everything that is contemplated is not what contemplates. Therefore, the body, feelings, or cognitions are not what contemplates.

In philosophical terms, the first three foundations are third-person knowledge of first-person experience, and the fourth is first-person knowledge of first-person experience. In conventional terms, these are the knowledge of the somatic, affective, and cognitive experience, and the knowledge of the phenomenological experience. Both perspectives coexist and are available at any time, although sometimes we adopt one perspective and sometimes the other. In the *Sutta*, we are urged to view each experience from both perspectives, and then from an integrated perspective.

Moreover, each phenomenon is contemplated when it enters the foreground of the experience, while it stays as the central phenomenon, and when it disappears. This is the most descriptive feature of *sati*. To be able to understand impermanence, conscious attention must be present when the phenomenon arises and accompany it until it disappears, with no interruption.

Understanding impermanence is more than just admitting that attention is unstable and jumps from one object to another. In fact, it's about recognizing that *there are no stable phenomena*, that everything is in a state of continuous flux, that everything that exists has a cycle, and therefore that it must cease to exist.

The refrain concludes by reminding us that direct physical sensations, feelings, and cognitions are necessary elements of knowledge and conscious attention. However, as they are impersonal and impermanent, attachment to them will produce dissatisfaction. To put it another way, none of them will provide permanent personal satisfaction.

So, the refrain reminds us that every area of experience it addresses has to be filtered and recognized as impersonal, impermanent, and unsatisfactory.

PART TWO

THE FOUR FOUNDATIONS OF ATTENTION
Sutta Study

1

CONTEMPLATION OF SOMATIC ACTIVITIES

> "Monks, I will teach you the unconditioned and the path leading to the unconditioned...."
> "And what, monks, is the unconditioned? The ending of desire, the ending of hatred, the ending of delusion: this is called the unconditioned."
> "And what, monks, is the path leading to the unconditioned? Mindfulness directed to the body: this is called the path leading to the unconditioned..."
> Parayana Sutta (Samyutta Nikaya 43, 44)

This chapter looks at achieving mindfulness through meditation on bodily experience—somatic activity—and how that approach is considered in the Sutta and through modern scientific understanding.

We understand "sensations" as being raw data (before it is evaluated) that reaches the receiving organ. We also want to differentiate sensations from the hedonic element that emotionally charges them. We try to break the word "feeling" into its two components, one physiological and the other affective, to make the cognitive process in the human species understandable.

The meditator must work on this immediate experience on its own terms—separate from whatever knowledge of anatomy or physiology they may have. The inability to do so can be an obstacle to directly experiencing the sensations.

The *Sutta* proposes that one should begin paying attention to the body by contemplating the breathing process as simple physical sensations in progress. Later, the contemplation is widened to the postures and movements of the body, eventually reaching the understanding that a whole series of somatic activities hidden from observation are taking place. The meditator understands that all physical sensations can be reduced to the four elements, in different combinations. The contemplation of the body ends with the understanding that the physical body is perishable and therefore that the release of dissatisfaction cannot be found there.

Sensations

When contemplating the first foundation of attention, the meditator focuses attention on the somatic experience. They discover a material body that can move in space and that functions due to a whole series of activities and processes that cannot be controlled voluntarily. The meditator inquires into the sensory receptors, deconstructing perception until they finally manage to break it down into its constituent sensory elements. The meditator recognizes the material elements that produce sensations and then perceives that these sensations are the result of contact between the object and the receiving organ. Therefore, the meditator understands that there is not only "something" but *also* "something else" that knows. Achieving this is the first knowledge of Vipassana, or the knowledge of *nama* (the mental) and *rupa* (the physical).

Satipatthāna Sutta: Contemplation of the Body
Mindfulness of Breathing

And how does a monk live contemplating the body in the body?

Herein, monks, a monk, having gone to the forest, to the foot of a tree or to an empty place, sits down with his legs crossed, keeps his body erect and his mindfulness alert.

Ever mindful he breathes in, mindful he breathes out. Breathing in a long breath, he knows, "I am breathing in a long breath;" breathing out a long breath, he knows, "I am breathing out a long breath;" breathing in a short breath, he knows, "I am breathing in a short breath;" breathing out a short breath, he knows, "I am breathing out a short breath."

"Experiencing the whole (breath-) body, I shall breathe in," thus he trains himself.

"Experiencing the whole (breath-) body, I shall breathe out," thus he trains himself. "Calming the activity of the (breath-) body, I shall breathe in," thus he trains himself. "Calming the activity of the (breath-) body, I shall breathe out," thus he trains himself.

Just as a skillful turner or turner's apprentice, making a long turn, knows, "I am making a long turn," or making a short turn, knows, "I am making a short turn," just so the monk, breathing in a long breath, knows, "I am breathing in a long breath;" breathing out a long breath, he knows, "I am breathing out a long breath;" breathing in a short breath, he knows, "I am breathing in a short breath;" breathing out a short breath, he knows, "I am breathing out a short breath." "Experiencing the whole (breath-) body, I shall breathe in," thus he trains himself. "Experiencing the whole (breath-) body, I shall breathe out," thus he trains himself. "Calming the activity of the (breath-) body, I shall breathe in," thus he trains himself. "Calming the activity of the (breath-) body, I shall breathe out," thus he trains himself.

Thus he lives contemplating the body in the body internally, or he lives contemplating the body in the body externally, or he lives contemplating the body in the body internally and externally. He lives contemplating origination factors in the body, or he lives contemplating dissolution factors in the body, or he lives contemplating origination-and-dissolution factors in the body. Or his mindfulness is established with the thought: "The body exists," to the extent necessary just for knowledge and mindfulness, and he lives detached, and clings to nothing in the world. Thus also, monks, a monk lives contemplating the body in the body.

The Four Postures
And further, monks, a monk knows, when he is going, "I am going;" he knows, when he is standing, "I am standing;" he knows, when he is sitting, "I am sitting;" he knows, when he is lying down, "I am lying down;" or just as his body is disposed so he knows it.

Thus he lives contemplating the body in the body internally, or he lives contemplating the body in the body externally, or he lives contemplating the body in the body internally and externally. He lives contemplating origination factors in the body, or he lives contemplating dissolution factors in the body, or he lives contemplating origination-and-dissolution factors in the body. Or his mindfulness is established with the thought: "The body exists," to the extent necessary just for knowledge and mindfulness, and he lives detached, and clings to nothing in the world. Thus also, monks, a monk lives contemplating the body in the body.

Mindfulness with Clear Comprehension
And further, monks, a monk, in going forward and back, applies clear comprehension; in looking straight on and looking away, he applies clear comprehension; in bending and in stretching, he applies clear comprehension; in wearing robes and carrying the bowl, he applies clear comprehension; in eating, drinking, chewing and savoring, he applies clear comprehension; in walking, in standing, in sitting, in falling asleep, in waking, in speaking and in keeping silence, he applies clear comprehension.

Thus he lives contemplating the body in the body...

Reflection on the Repulsiveness of the Body
And further, monks, a monk reflects on this very body enveloped by the skin and full of manifold impurity, from the soles up, and from the top of the head-hairs down, thinking thus: "There are in this body hair of the head, hair of the body, nails, teeth, skin, flesh, sinews, bones, marrow, kidney, heart, liver,

midriff, spleen, lungs, intestines, mesentery, gorge, feces, bile, phlegm, pus, blood, sweat, fat, tears, grease, saliva, nasal mucus, synovial fluid, urine."

Just as if there were a double-mouthed provision bag full of various kinds of grain such as hill paddy, paddy, green gram, cow-peas, sesamum, and husked rice, and a man with sound eyes, having opened that bag, were to take stock of the contents thus: "This is hill paddy, this is paddy, this is green gram, this is cow-pea, this is sesamum, this is husked rice." Just so, monks, a monk reflects on this very body enveloped by the skin and full of manifold impurity, from the soles up, and from the top of the head-hairs down, thinking thus: "There are in this body hair of the head, hair of the body, nails, teeth, skin, flesh, sinews, bones, marrow, kidney, heart, liver, midriff, spleen, lungs, intestines, mesentery, gorge, feces, bile, phlegm, pus, blood, sweat, fat, tears, grease, saliva, nasal mucus, synovial fluid, urine."

Thus he lives contemplating the body in the body...

Reflection on the Material Elements

And further, monks, a monk reflects on this very body, however it be placed or disposed, by way of the material elements: "There are in this body the element of earth, the element of water, the element of fire, the element of wind."

Just as if, monks, a clever cow-butcher or his apprentice, having slaughtered a cow and divided it into portions, should be sitting at the junction of four high roads, in the same way, a monk reflects on this very body, as it is placed or disposed, by way of the material elements: "There are in this body the elements of earth, water, fire, and wind."

Thus he lives contemplating the body in the body...

The Nine Cemetery Contemplations

And further, monks, as if a monk sees a body dead one, two, or three days; swollen, blue and festering, thrown in the charnel ground, he then applies this perception to his own body thus: "Verily, also my own body is of the same nature; such it will become and will not escape it."

Thus he lives contemplating the body in the body internally, or he lives contemplating the body in the body externally, or he lives contemplating the body in the body internally and externally. He lives contemplating origination-factors in the body, or he lives contemplating dissolution factors in the body, or he lives contemplating origination-and-dissolution-factors in the body. Or his mindfulness is established with the thought: "The body exists," to the extent necessary just for knowledge and mindfulness, and he lives detached, and clings to nothing in the world. Thus also, monks, a monk lives contemplating the body in the body.

And further, monks, as if a monk sees a body thrown in the charnel ground, being eaten by crows, hawks, vultures, dogs, jackals or by different kinds of worms, he then applies this perception to his own body thus: "Verily, also my own body is of the same nature; such it will become and will not escape it."

Thus he lives contemplating the body in the body...

And further, monks, as if a monk sees a body thrown in the charnel ground and reduced to a skeleton with some flesh and blood attached to it, held together by the tendons...

And further, monks, as if a monk sees a body thrown in the charnel ground and reduced to a skeleton blood-besmeared and without flesh, held together by the tendons...

And further, monks, as if a monk sees a body thrown in the charnel ground and reduced to a skeleton without flesh and blood, held together by the tendons...

And further, monks, as if a monk sees a body thrown in the charnel ground and reduced to disconnected bones, scattered in all directions here a bone of the hand, there a bone of the foot, a shin bone, a thigh bone, the pelvis, spine and skull...

And further, monks, as if a monk sees a body thrown in the charnel ground, reduced to bleached bones of conch-like color...

And further, monks, as if a monk sees a body thrown in the charnel ground reduced to bones, more than a year-old, lying in a heap...

And further, monks, as if a monk sees a body thrown in the charnel ground, reduced to bones gone rotten and become dust, he then applies this perception to his own body thus: "Verily, also my own body is of the same nature; such it will become and will not escape it."

Thus he lives contemplating the body in the body internally, or he lives contemplating the body in the body externally, or he lives contemplating the body in the body internally and externally. He lives contemplating origination factors in the body, or he lives contemplating dissolution factors in the body, or he lives contemplating origination-and-dissolution factors in the body. Or his mindfulness is established with the thought: "The body exists," to the extent necessary just for knowledge and mindfulness, and he lives detached, and clings to nothing in the world. Thus also, monks, a monk lives contemplating the body in the body.

Meditation

The first paragraph of this section of the *Sutta* begins by giving the basic instructions for meditation. Let us remember that the Buddhist worldview does not look externally to find the solution to suffering, but rather finds it in lived experience. Nevertheless, human experience is both complex and dizzying. It is also dispersed and partial, and this lies at the root of ignorance, hence dissatisfaction. We experience many different things at high speed. To cope with these characteristics of experience we build an experimental situation that allows us to understand its operation: meditation.

Meditation is a ritual procedure, and its objective is to modify our normal state of consciousness through voluntary attention control. As in other methods of modifying consciousness, set and setting must be established. *Set* is the mental state that a person brings to experience—the thoughts, mood, and expectations. *Setting* is the physical and social environment.

As we have already said, to understand how experience really works and, consequently, to be able to free ourselves from dissatisfaction, Buddhism proposes a method called the "Noble Eightfold Path." This method can be summarized in three basic areas that must be developed: *Sila* (moral conduct), *Samadhi* (cognition) and *Paññā* (intention). Benefits can likely be obtained from any of them, but liberation requires all three. This is why meditation creates a situation that includes all these three areas.

Paññā (correct understanding and correct intention) constitutes the *set* of meditative practice. Meditation is not practiced in order to be a better person or to resolve personal problems, nor to find relaxation or disconnection from the everyday world, nor even to reach a certain state of concentration or well-being. Instead, one sits down to meditate to investigate how dissatisfaction figures in one's own experience—what its origins are and how it may cease. Of course, this intention is difficult to maintain, and other intentions will inevitably divert us from the path.

Sila (correct or healthy action, speech, and way of life) constitutes the *setting* for meditative practice. This can be achieved by restricting physical and verbal behavior, specifically, through immobility and silence. Under these conditions, one cannot carry out any unethical action. Ethics in *Dhamma* are functional—that is to say, if I do this or that, I suffer bad consequences. But if I do not do it, there are no bad consequences (by which we mean bad immediate consequences, i.e. more agitation or a proliferation of emotions and thoughts and, consequently, less calm or less peace).

This paragraph of the *Sutta* talks of finding a secluded place, with few stimuli, and of adopting a static and vertical posture. Immobility prevents the active search for sensual pleasure; verticality, apart from being the natural position of the human body, is what allows for the proper functioning of the attentional systems.

The "meditation stage" is completed with voluntary attention modification. Traditionally, two methods are used: voluntarily directing and sustaining attention towards an "object;" or directing and sustaining attention on one's own attention (what is today known as *open monitoring*, a form of meta-attention).

Meditation "objects" may be external entities such as elements of nature, water, earth, air, or fire; they may be a particular quality, such as color; or they may be other fundamental elements, such as space or light. You can also use concepts, such as the human qualities of goodness, joy, compassion, or composure; perceptions, such as pleasant or disgusting aspects of the human body; even reflections, which imply an intensive application of thought. This way of meditating has a primary "object." All attention is directed towards the chosen object, thus causing a predetermined state of consciousness. Nowadays these meditations are called "generative practices" because their objective is to generate a particular state of consciousness.

Meta-attentional practices consist of paying attention to changes in attention. Observing the spontaneous process in the experience, the meditator discovers its rhythms and regularities, heeding changes in intensity and speed, as well as the relationships between phenomena as they arise and disperse. The concentration or dispersion of the focus is one of the dimensions addressed by meta-attention.

Therefore, the "meditative scene" is an experimental situation that the Noble Eightfold Path recreates: the control of *Sila* and the development of *Pañña* serve to deepen *Samadhi* during meditation (*bhavana* or development of the body/mind). In meditation, one develops a state of harmonized intention, action, and cognition that becomes more stable and long lasting until it can be properly maintained throughout practical daily activities.

In the tradition of the Buddha, *samatha* (concentration meditation) and Vipassana (open monitoring meditation) are practices necessary for mental stability, but when one follows *Satipatthāna*, *sati* is the precursor and *samadhi* the consequence. The major contribution that the Buddha's tradition makes is to show that concentration is needed moment by moment, which is different than fixed concentration. The important thing is to view the process, not to stop it. *Sati* and *samadhi* are components of the attention system. By practicing Vipassana, you gain knowledge because there is awareness of the changes that affect observation, but when practicing *samatha*, you gain mental calmness because awareness of change is inhibited, forcing the observation to be fixed. Instead of being mutually exclusive, these two systems of meditation techniques should be developed in parallel.

Sati and *samadhi* are invisible because they are qualities of attention paid to each and every moment. To understand this, we will have to change the scale at which we observe experience. What we call "the present" is a scale that is too large for us to understand how attention works. The present is made up of myriad moments of attention, and each one has its own *sati*, *samadhi*, and *vayama*. *Sati* is attention moment by moment, *samadhi* is concentration of the attentional resources on each moment, and *vayama* is the level of alertness at each moment. *Sati* monitors the orientation and focus of attention, while *samadhi* pays full attention to what occupies the attentional focus.

> **Experience is complex and dizzying, and attention is the way to embrace it.**

Neither *sati* nor *samadhi* start out fully developed—indeed, they are cognitive activities that have to be trained. The paradox is that they are trained to contemplate each phenomenon and each moment of consciousness as if it were the first time, using the slow, controlled, explicit, conscious, "in series" processing style.

A traditional way of describing the development of *samadhi* is the "ten stages of *Kamalashila*"; to develop *sati*, the "sixteen levels of Vipassana knowledge" is often used. (See Figures 5 and 6.)

Stage	Name	Mental State	Relation to Object	Type of Attention
1	Directed	Wandering and agitated	Superficial	Not sustained
2	Preparatory	Calmer	Initial clarity	Sustained
3	Initial	More focused	Direct experience	Sustained and constant
4	Unified	Fully focused	Mind-object fusion	Sustained, constant and deep
5	Peaceful	Peaceful and balanced	Complete integration	Sustained, constant, deep and peaceful
6	Inner calm	Calm and stable	Deep knowledge	Sustained, constant, deep, peaceful and unified
7	Mentally strong	Strong and firm	Total clarity	Sustained, constant, deep, peaceful, unified and stable
8	Unidirectional	Focused and unidirectional	Total absorption	Sustained, constant, deep, peaceful, unified, stable and unidirectional
9	Equable	Balanced and equanimous	Mind-object balance	Sustained, constant, deep, peaceful, unified, stable, unidirectional and equanimous
10	Mindful	Fully conscious	Absolute clarity	Sustained, constant, deep, peaceful, unified, stable, unidirectional, equanimous and fully conscious

Figure 5: A schematic representation of Kamalashila's ten stages of attention.

First Vipassana Jhana	1. Insight knowledge of discerning mind and matter (*namarupa pariccheda nana*).
	2. Insight knowledge of causal relations between mental and physical states (*paccaya pariggaha nana*).
	3. Insight knowledge of the mental and physical processes as impermanent and unsatisfactory (*sammasana nana*).
Second Vipassana Jhana	4. Insight knowledge of arising and passing away of all phenomena (*udayabbaya nana*).
Third Vipassana Jhana	5. Insight knowledge of dissolution (*bhanga nana*).
	6. Insight knowledge of fearfulness (*bhaya nana*).
	7. Insight knowledge of the dangers of mental and physical states (*adinava nana*).
	8. Insight knowledge of disgust (*nibbida nana*).
	9. Insight knowledge of desire of deliverance from the mundane (*uncitukamayata nana*).
	10. Insight knowledge of the path to liberation and the decision to practice more (*patisankha nana*).
Fourth-Eighth Vipassana Jhanas	11. Insight knowledge of equanimity of the mental and physical states (*sankharupekha nana*).
	12. Insight knowledge of the Four Noble Truths (*anuloma nana*).
	13. Insight knowledge of liberation from the mundane (*gotrabhu nana*).
	14. Insight knowledge of the abandonment and destruction of impurities (*magga nana*).
Immaterial Vipassana Jhanas	15. Insight knowledge of the fruits of the path and which has nibbana as the goal (*phala nana*).
	16. Insight knowledge of the remaining impurities (*paccavekkhana nana*).

Figure 6: The sixteen insights of Vipassana.

Experience is complex and dizzying, and attention is the way to embrace it. Meditation is a technology that develops these qualities of attention, rather than those of the observer or the observed.

The Buddha's discovery is that you can construct ecstatic states of consciousness by absorption in healthy objects, but unless you deconstruct the mind that has been conditioned by a history of reinforcements and by all the decisions that have constructed personality, it is impossible to maintain these states. Furthermore, the conditioned mind is prey to programming that goes beyond one's own biography, and that is shared with many other animal species.

The aim of the Buddha's form of meditation as we understand it is not so much for the subject to disappear into moments of "non-duality," but rather for it be realized that there is no subject to begin with. To this end, all conditioning has to be patiently deconstructed through meta-attentional presence, which is what provides the "vision" of how one's own existence as subject originates. This wisdom allows the meditator to see that existing as a subject is precisely the origin of existential dissatisfaction.

To sum up, the Buddha's form of meditation consists of cultivating a system of conscious attention to experience in which *sati*, *samadhi*, and *vayama* serve to control the lens used for observation. Nevertheless, the metaphor of the lens is insufficient because *sati* not only heeds the continuous change of focus (impermanence) but also the continuous change of affective tone (dissatisfaction) and intentionality, and consequently of subject or agent that may be considered "the observer" (impersonality).

> What does not know does not suffer. Therefore, the origin of suffering can only be in what knows.

Matter

Our starting point for understanding matter in the Vipassana sense is that we have a body. In the *Sutta* there are six sections dedicated to somatic experience. Although *sati* has to learn to be present in any change that occurs in any of the four registers (somatic experience, affective experience, cognitive experience, and phenomenological experience), the observation of physical phenomena is easier because they are more consistent than evanescent mental phenomena. They are also the privileged area where we can discriminate between *what knows* and *what does not know*.

Experience is made up of something that knows and something that is known. It is not that the material elements are not aware of themselves, which is a very sophisticated result of evolution, but that, being practically inert, they do not seek anything, nor do they react to external circumstances or undergo transformations. What does not know does not suffer. Therefore, the origin of suffering can only be in what knows. The Buddha's method does not reduce experience to the interaction between material elements, nor is it interested in physiological explanations that are not part of the first-person experience. The *Sutta* offers different somatic activities that can be observed. Somatic regulation is learned through detached observation. (See Figure 7.)

FOCUS	WHAT AND HOW TO OBSERVE	
Breathing	Awareness of process Observation of process	Feeling the body Calming the body
Proprioception	Walking Standing	Sitting Lying
Interoception	Orientation Stillness/Movement	Sleep/Wakefulness Inaction/Action
Physiological Activities	Fluids and waste Hair and nails	Skin: texture, layer, tone
Elements	Solidity Cohesion	Temperature Pressure
Dispersion of Matter	Nature of the body, degradation and disintegration	

Figure 7: How to observe somatic activity.

Attention to Breathing

The *Sutta* begins the section on conscious attention to the body by focusing on breathing. Conscious attention must extend to all the processes of human life, including the body and the breath. The body is subject to a process of continuous change, and the respiratory process is a physiological one that is consubstantial with the bodily cycle. There is breathing all the time—it never ceases from birth to death—and it is easily observable. Being a "bottom-up" physiological process, breathing is easily distinguishable from "top-down" mental activities. It is a non-conceptual process, something that can be experienced directly without having to think. Breathing is a vital activity in constant flux.

It must be said that of the different written versions of the *Sutta* that exist, the oldest ones did not include attention to breath (*anapanasati*). On the other hand, we do know that attention to breath had a fundamental influence on the Buddha's spiritual development. His first meditation teacher, Arada Kamala, taught him the practice of concentration

Integral Vipassana

on breathing, reaching the four material absorptions or *jhanas*, while his second teacher, Udaka Ramaputta, led him to the "sphere of perception-no perception," the highest level of mental abstraction that could be accessed by meditation at that time.

However, the Buddha did not find in these states the answer to his existential dilemma. He left the path of concentration to dedicate himself to the ascetic path, before finding the "middle way" that led to his awakening. Nevertheless, he taught attention to breath as a fundamental element of his method, as long as it's accompanied by *sati*. In many *suttas*, reference is made to *anapanasati*. *Anapana* refers to the in and out of breath during respiration. It is a yogic practice to which Buddha adds *sati*—that is to say, conscious attention to breathing.

The *Anapanasati Sutta*, the discourse on conscious attention to breathing, states that "the cultivation of conscious attention to breathing is very fruitful and very beneficial. When conscious attention to breath is developed and cultivated, the four forms of conscious attention are perfected. When the four forms of conscious attention *are developed and cultivated, the seven factors of illumination are perfected.*" This may be the reason for including the first section of the practice of conscious attention to breath (*anapanasati*) in the *Satipatthāna*.

> **When we pay attention to breathing, we are in the present.**

Breathing is normally an involuntary process, but it is affected by the continual changes of activity of the organism in general, and by mental activity in particular. Voluntary activity itself can slow it down or speed it up. As a result, it is constantly "torn between" the voluntary and the involuntary. It is also the interchange between the internal and external worlds, between giving and receiving, between the "I" and "the other." In addition, breathing is a process that happens here and now. This is why it is a guarantee that, when we pay attention to breathing, we are in the present and paying conscious attention to that moment. This is the first step of attention to breath, knowing when there is *sati* and when there is not.

Normally, having to pay attention to something brings with it assessments and value judgments that make us voluntarily intervene in the process. However, here this is not necessarily a bad thing, precisely because we are using breath as an opportunity to observe the interference caused by mental processes. We find ourselves with our breathing, and this includes the part of us that wants to control our breathing, as well as the part of us that wants to stop controlling it. This is where the learning takes place. Here the meditator discovers how to undo that knot and reach the point that the breathing process occurs at its own pace and without feeling the urge to control it. In this way we become aware of our compulsion to control, or of the underlying belief that the "I" controls and directs the organism. This is the second step of attention to breathing.

At first, paying attention to the breath can be boring for us, and we quickly switch to "autopilot"—but the deeper we go, the more we become aware of the infinite variety that makes each and every inhalation and exhalation different. Each breath has a beginning, a middle, and an end. Each inhalation goes through a process of birth, growth, and death, and each exhalation does exactly the same. The depth and speed of breathing change according to our emotional state, our thoughts, and external circumstances. There is breathing and what is realized about breathing. There is a physiological process and what you realize about the process, a body and a mind, all interacting. Actually, everything is here. This is the third step of attention to breathing.

The narrator, that character created to make the experience understandable and relatable, will tend to comment on the process. You have to realize that this is how thinking works. Sometimes those comments will be of frustration, boredom, or surfeit, but we must peer underneath to see the affective activity of attachment to, or rejection of, what is happening. Sometimes, lethargy will appear; other times, restlessness. The meditator must realize that all of these are "obstacles" or "hindrances" to mental stability. It is important to realize that when too much effort goes into concentration, the result is a lack of mental stability. This is the fourth step of conscious attention to breathing.

When practicing *sati*, or conscious attention, what interests us is the tactile sensation of air entering and leaving our body. We are interested in the physical sensation of breathing, the feeling of the air impacting somewhere in the body. As this can be ambiguous, we will have to choose a particular point—the more concrete and limited the better—to focus on feeling that physical sensation. We are not interested in breathing as an object of concentration but as a means to develop conscious attention to physical sensations. Through breathing, we can quiet physiological activities so that the attention system can function better moment by moment.

Attention to the breath process begins with discriminating when there is *sati* and when there is not. When we practice *Satipatthāna*, breathing is both a reference point and a refuge to recognize the presence or absence of *sati*. The second step is to observe the respiratory process without voluntary intervention. As has been explained, when attention is obedient to the intention of the "I," it cannot focus on the observation of the physiological process as it really is at each moment. The third is to prioritize the somatic experience over the other activities—in other words, to attend only to physical experiences. When we do this, we are alone in the somatic experience and attentive to it. We recognize the vertiginous process of body and mind interacting. The fourth is to realize that when directing attention to a single register, physiological calm is deeper. This is what the *Anapanasati Sutta* means by affirming that the cultivation of conscious attention to respiration is "very fruitful and very beneficial" because, thanks to it, the four forms of conscious attention are perfected. From now on, physiological calm will be the reference point to confirm that *samadhi* and *vayama* are fulfilling their role in the realization of *Samadhi*.

Following the instructions given in the definition, *sati* has to observe "the body as body"—that is to say, the *somatic experience*. This must occur with the attentional alert network that looks after regulating the activity of the physiological organism, with no interference from the orientation network that manages the strength of desire (attraction or repulsion) or from the executive network which deals with intention and cognitive interpretation. Through the practice of attention to breathing, *sati* is trained as proposed in the definition—that is, we *know* whether it is activated or not, whether it realizes what is happening from moment to moment, and whether there are oscillations in desire or in dissatisfaction (*atapi, sampajañña* and *vineyya loke abhijjha domanassam*).

The aim is to maintain attention throughout the whole process of inhalation, exhalation, and the pauses between the one and the other. However, the other two "top-down" regulatory systems interfere because they have their own habits. They cause somatic, affective, and cognitive interference— modifications and preferences that impede the ability to pay attention to the respiratory process. The result is that when there is no *sati*, there is a surge in thoughts, evaluations, and activation changes in the organism. By trying to guide and focus attentional resources towards a single process, we are altering the organism's attention habits, which will tend to copy its rhythms and regularities. These are what we call *obstacles*. However, they are not distractions, but rather the process of a conditioned mind, and thanks to *sati* they reveal themselves in the only order that allows for their deconditioning.

Through attention to breathing, we develop the *samadhi* and *vayama* suitable for cultivating *sati*. In fact, once this point is reached, the meditator may opt to follow "the path of serenity" or "the path of wisdom." The *samatha yanika* focuses attention on breathing while the *vipassana yanika* develops *samadhi* through conscious attention (*sati*) to all the body's activities.

In fact, attention to breathing is a technical resource for developing wisdom, but its introduction in the *Satipatthāna* breaks, in a certain manner, the logic of the *Sutta*.

As we have noted, the first foundation of attention is dedicated to what we call somatic activities or sensations, which correspond to *rupa* in Pali, and which is usually translated as materiality. While the rest of the sections of this first foundation are clearly directed towards these type of activities, attention to breath seems to have the function of introducing the instructions on how to practice *Samatha* meditation, rather than of Vipassana contemplation. Learning how to cling to an object such as breathing while, at the same time, working on the process of releasing this attachment, introduces some contradiction into the *Sutta* that has affected its reception and generated endless debate.

Proprioception

In the *Sutta*, *sati* next focuses on the position of the body in space, what we today call *proprioception*. Through *sati*, the first thing the meditator discovers is that there is a body moving in space and, therefore, that there is activity by material within another material. In addition, *sati* realizes that there is an experience of the body in space—and also that it may be aware of that experience, or not. When there is conscious attention, the meditator knows the body is seated, but there are many times they do not know this. On many occasions, one is not aware of where the body is in space, nor of what the body is doing. Many movements are carried out mechanically while thinking or performing another mental activity. Although at all times there is a body and a bodily experience, sometimes there is *sati* and sometimes there is not. To put it another way, sometimes there is conscious attention and sometimes there is none.

Yet again, the Buddha's insight surprises us. Proprioception is a complex but fundamental system for human beings because it is in charge of knowing, at every moment, not only the position of the body or its parts, but also its balance, the speed and direction of its movement, and the degree of tension in its muscles and joints. Thanks to proprioception, we can adjust the force we use to grasp an object, alter the timing of a movement, or note a change in weight. We can jump, push, hit, collide with, or throw objects.

> An increase in body awareness is one of the benefits most proven by current research into mindfulness.

Moreover, we get feedback from the movements and the motor patterns the body is performing. All this is coordinated by the vestibular system, responsible for maintaining balance, taking into account the force of gravity, and controlling the gaze and keeping us upright when in motion—for instance, when going down stairs.

Proprioception is a subcategory of the more global classification of somatic sensations or *somato-sensations*. There are schools of meditation in motion which develop this quality, such as Yoga, Tai Chi, or the Feldenkrais Method. When proprioception is poorly developed, the body shows little fluidity of movement, is clumsy, has poor muscle tone, and has a tendency to fall over or to miscalculate distances. Underdeveloped proprioception indicates that the body's experience in space is not well integrated with the organism's other activities.

An increase in body awareness is one of the benefits most proven by current research into mindfulness. In fact, a whole new trend in mindfulness movement, called "embodiment," deals with these aspects.

A body-mind dissociation is at the root of many mental illnesses. The mind dissociates itself from its material support but loses itself in a mental world stripped of biological limits.

Be that as it may, the key to the paragraph lies in the word "know." ("He knows, when he is standing, 'I am standing.'"). Once again we have a double perspective: something known and something that knows, the body (*rupa*) and the somatic experience (*nama*). But additionally, there is the *metaconscious* vision that is aware of both. This metaconscious awareness is the first insight of Vipassana and is called *namarupa*.

Interoception

That same understanding can be extended to the rest of external somatic activities, revealing to us that in all of them there is a body (*rupa*) and an activity (*nama*). The material body does not move alone; it moves because something decides to move it. That something is *nama*, mental activities. The keyword of this paragraph is lucidity (*sampajañña*), which is a question of applying the insight of *namarupa* to all external activities of the body. To put it another way, we must consciously grasp that the body (*rupa*) moves the gaze (*nama*) from one side to the other, and be aware that the body (*rupa*) changes its position (*nama*), whether getting dressed, or drinking, or eating, or defecating. There is always the body (*rupa*) and the action (*nama*). The same applies when sleeping or waking up. The body and the activity of sleeping, the body and the activity of awakening. The body and the activity of speaking, the body and the activity of being silent.

That daily activities are mentioned reminds us that *Satipatthāna* practice should be extended beyond the moments of formal meditation. That is why Vipassana is observed in retreats lasting several days, where formal practice alternates with basic existence.

In modern mindfulness, "informal practice" urges us to pay conscious attention to somatic activities such as driving, brushing teeth, or cooking. This is the most valued aspect in mindfulness when applied to work, as the intention here is not so much to escape from dissatisfaction but rather to improve performance and productivity. Strictly speaking, what is known today as the "informal practice" of mindfulness is in fact the traditional "formal practice."

Physiological Activities

The next paragraph in the *Sutta* deals with the rest of the body's activities that normally go unnoticed. The experience of contact leads to contemplation of the body's internal activities. This is what today we call *interoception* and refers to activities that do not require conscious mediation, for example the functioning of organs, fluids, and wastes. We are not generally aware of the functioning of the integumentary system that comprises the skin, hair, nails, subcutaneous tissue, sweat glands, sebaceous glands, ceruminous, or mammary glands, which all have important functions for the body's balance.

In this case, at the same time that we focus attention on these activities, we understand that the *namarupa* relationship is profoundly intertwined with all physiological activity. It is not a question of making how it works conscious, but rather about recognizing that there are many activities that the organism (*namarupa*) performs without our being aware. Yet again, the aim of *Satipatthāna* is not body control, as in yoga or ascetic practices, but rather to develop conscious attention to the point of being able to understand how dissatisfaction functions. In this sense, the paragraph has the role of pointing out that the body/mind performs unconscious processes and that, consequently, there is nobody in charge. Accepting this lack of control undoes the illusion of "I am the body" or "this is my body." In the end, if I were the body, I would know what it is doing at all moments; if it were mine, the body would not do so many things that I find unpleasant.

This *Sutta* paragraph refers to the body "as a bag of groceries with two openings." The body is scanned "up-down" and "down-up," and it is discovered that there are many elements to the body that are not visible nor capable of being experienced during the contemplation of the body, even though we know that they are there and that they perform a function not governed by anybody beyond the organism itself.

The Elements

We must remember that empirical observation is the only tool used in contemplation. Bearing this in mind, awareness can only extend to the indivisible qualities of the experience of matter—its degree of solidity or malleability, its fluidity or cohesion, its temperature and pressure. These fundamental qualities of somatic experience can be viewed internally as phenomenological qualities, or externally, as the butcher does in the *Sutta*, discovering that the body is flesh, liquid, temperature, and air—the four material elements of Hindu tradition. But it can also be experienced internally *and* externally, understanding that they are two aspects of the same thing.

A stone can be known both as matter and as a psychological experience that includes not only tactile awareness but also other physical sensations such as form and color, and mental activities such as name or concept. The same goes for a feeling or a thought. They can be seen from both perspectives—as a physiological activity and as a psychological experience—knowing that both coexist. You can try to explain the physiological activity as chemical and electrical activity in a physical body, but in that case, we would no longer be in the field of experience.

The simile of the butcher is used because at that time he was the one who cut up bodies, but the choice of this word is not intended to reduce the knowledge of matter to solely chemistry, physics, or organic biology. This knowledge is not the result of empirical observations, but of subtle manipulations by researchers. In the *Sutta*, the psychological is not reduced to its biological correlate, but neither is it a stable or permanent subject constructed from biographical and contextual intentions or circumstances. It may be that, employing certain procedures, when we feel sad, we could observe a serotonin deficiency—but then we would not be using the Buddha's method. Sadness is not the activity of matter, but the name for a mental experience that includes a history of reinforcements of similar moments the organism has experienced. Sometimes we "are aware" of it, and at other times we "are not aware," and there is only the experience of sadness.

> **Matter and mind are two aspects of the same thing, and there is nothing more than those two perspectives interacting.**

It is such a profound insight that it has a considerable influence on the process of detachment from the body and from "I," which all started with the understanding that "I" cannot control breathing, movements that occur in the body, bodily activities, or the basic functioning of the organism.

The understanding of *namarupa* is deepened thanks to the experience that *rupa* is just matter and, therefore, is not what knows. In fact, what knows is what is aware of matter and its activity. Again, the only tool used for contemplating reality is the observation of one's own experience. This understanding does not require *thinking* about it; all that is needed is the *knowledge* that there is a body, along with enough conscious attention to continuously maintain this awareness that there is a body. Meditation is not a work of introspection but of contemplation. In that observation, one experiences a frenetic activity of thoughts, feelings, and sensations. Attention is directed to any of the activities spelled out by the *Sutta* (breathing, bodily position, body movements) even though we know that many other bodily activities cannot be consciously experienced. We understand that here there is a body with all its activities and a mind that experiences, and that they are interdependent.

The Dispersion of Matter

If in the simile of the butcher a corpse appears for the first time, even if it is just of an animal, the self realizes that this will also be its destiny. Recognizing that there is a process of bodily decomposition in which the four elements disperse, we understand that any being with a body will undergo that same process. The body is a process that has a beginning and an end, and it can be seen as matter identical to the matter that surrounds it. Mortality can then be faced as the final destiny of all beings that are born, develop, grow old, and die—in other words, all impermanent beings. Contemplation of the first foundation of attention leads us to the understanding, still immature, of impermanence as a characteristic of everything that has biological existence.

In Summary

The first foundation of attention is what we have called *somatic activities* or sensation, and it is composed of the ways the organism collects information. Sensation is the basic experience of stimulation from the senses. It is "bottom-up" processing, detecting something through the senses (sight, hearing, taste, smell, and touch) and the internal sensing receptors (movement, balance, tension) before it's been elaborated upon or given meaning.

The human body is equipped with specialized systems for obtaining information. These are called senses, or sensory systems, and register changes in environmental energy. The energy that reaches a receptor must be sufficiently intense as to cause a noticeable effect. The intensity of physical energy needed to produce a sensation is called the *absolute threshold*. The absolute threshold exists between the minimum amount of stimulus needed to fire up cognitive activity (the lower threshold) and the maximum amount of stimulus that can be received (the upper limit). *The differential threshold* is the minimum detectable change and varies from one organism to another and from one moment to another.

Examined from the *Sutta's* perspective, the organism has exteroceptive sensors, which inform us of the outside world (sight, taste, hearing, touch, smell); interoceptors, which receive information from inside the organism; and proprioceptors, which monitor the movement and condition of muscles, joints (kinaesthesia), and balance (vestibular). Consequently, when cultivating *sati* we are urged to experience all sensations lucidly—visual, auditory, olfactory, gustatory, tactile, thermal, kinaesthetic, and those of orientation and balance. "Lucidly" here means realizing that sensation is the product of contact between the receptor and its object, and that both are matter (*rupa*). It also means being conscious of the experience of that contact (*nama*). Contemplation without moments of neglect (*sati*) of somatic activities leads to the discovery that one cannot exist without the other (*namarupa*). Let there be no doubt that "there is a body," as well as that knowledge and attention are necessary.

2

CONTEMPLATION OF THE ACTIVITIES OF FEELING

> *"To be aware of the feelings without any ego reference will also help to distinguish them clearly from the physical stimuli arousing them, as well as from the subsequent mental reactions to them. Thereby the meditator will be able to keep his attention focused on the feelings alone, without straying into other areas. This is the purport of the phrase 'he contemplates feelings in the feelings' as stated in the Satipatthāna Sutta."*
> —Contemplation of Feeling, Nyanaponika Thera, 1995

This chapter explains how the *Sutta* guides us to observe bodily experience, breathing, posture, body movement in space, and other sensations. Modern science and psychology can help us understand the importance of these activities.

The meditator finds that what brings them out of immobility are non-conscious or non-voluntary reactions to physical discomfort. Sometimes there is movement without having made the decision to move. Other times the discomfort or pain takes control and, despite attempts not to move, the discomfort becomes unbearable, and you end up changing posture. Now comes the understanding that the body avoids pain or that the mind is dominated by it. Physical sensations are always accompanied by feelings, which are not a characteristic of the object but an activity of the subject. Matter does not feel, what feels is the mind.

By "feeling activities," we mean those activities that evaluate from a hedonic point of view sensations such as pleasure, pain, or neither pleasure nor pain. This qualitative procedure is what makes the organism react and look for affective balance. Vedana, or affective evaluation, is the body's response to any stimulus. The stimulus, a product of contact between a sensory base and its object, generates an intention to approach and retain, or move away and avoid. This contact, I like or I don't like. Remember that the intellect is, for the *Dhamma*, just one more sense. Put another way, if a pleasant memory arises in the mind, the organism (body/mind) will tend to seek it out or repeat it. If the memory is painful, the organism will tend to avoid it and generate aversion towards it.

Thus, we see that the activities of feeling are the origin of dissatisfaction.

This chapter provides questions to ponder and ways to work with the feeling activities. The relationship between desire and attachment is revealed, continuity between the innate and the acquired is proposed, and the relationship between learning and conditioning is revealed. Finally, the pursuit of pleasure and the avoidance of pain is seen to be the mechanism by which the "I" comes about.

Feeling

When contemplating the second foundation of attention, the meditator directs attention towards pleasure and pain in somatic activities, as well as towards what is pleasant and unpleasant in mental activities.

Physical sensations appear attached to the activity of feeling and, in the same way, mental sensations—images, representations, symbols, ideas, concepts, and language—also emerge attached to the activity of feeling.

The meditator contemplates the qualities of these physical sensations—solidity, intensity, shape, cohesion, pressure, temperature, and any other sensation or contact by a sensory organ with its objects—until they discover that pleasure or pain are not inherent to physical sensations. In the same way, the meditator contemplates mental sensations and discovers that there is nothing in them that is inherently pleasant or unpleasant. It is understood that when there is feeling associated with sensations, there emerges a tendency to apprehend or avoid, a longing identified as desire. Desire or dissatisfaction (thirst in Pali) has an urge to be filled, which sets in motion an automatic reaction that tries to fill that void with objects or conditioned activities (fuel in Pali). These can reduce or increase desire. In the first case, what is left of the desire will lead to a continuation of the search for satisfaction. In the second, a proliferation of activities will arise that will only increase agitation and unease.

This endless process allows the meditator to realize that all reactions have consequences, thereby revealing a first understanding of the law of cause and effect.

Satipatthāna Sutta: Contemplation of Feeling

And how, monks, does a monk live contemplating feelings in feelings?

Herein, monks, a monk when experiencing a pleasant feeling knows, "I experience a pleasant feeling;" when experiencing a painful feeling, he knows, "I experience a painful feeling;" when experiencing a neither-pleasant-nor-painful feeling," he knows, "I experience a neither-pleasant-nor-painful feeling." When experiencing a pleasant worldly feeling, he knows, "I experience a pleasant worldly feeling;" when experiencing a pleasant spiritual feeling, he knows, "I experience a pleasant spiritual feeling;" when experiencing a painful worldly feeling, he knows, "I experience a painful worldly feeling;" when experiencing a painful spiritual feeling, he knows, "I experience a painful spiritual feeling;" when experiencing a neither-pleasant-nor-painful worldly feeling, he knows, "I experience a neither-pleasant-nor-painful worldly feeling;" when experiencing a neither-pleasant-nor-painful spiritual feeling, he knows, "I experience a neither-pleasant-nor-painful spiritual feeling."

Thus he lives contemplating feelings in feelings internally, or he lives contemplating feelings in feelings externally, or he lives contemplating feelings in feelings internally and externally. He lives contemplating origination factors in feelings, or he lives contemplating dissolution factors in feelings, or he lives contemplating origination-and-dissolution factors in feelings. Or his mindfulness is established with the thought, "Feeling exists," to the extent necessary just for knowledge and mindfulness, and he lives detached, and clings to nothing in the world. Thus, monks, a monk lives contemplating feelings in feelings.

From Sensations to Feelings

Normally, when we talk about sensations, we view them as good or bad. The immediacy between the sensory contact and the emotional evaluation, or feeling, leads us to believe that they are the same. In the *Dhamma* each contact has its corresponding assessment, while in daily life we believe that the emotional, sentimental, or affective only happens occasionally. In the Buddha's method, each and every contact between object and sensory base produces a mental activity of feeling. The second foundation of attention is feeling.

In the first foundation, the knot of *nama* and *rupa* is undone when we understand that both the object and the sensory base are *rupa*. *Nama* is the experience of the contact and also the awareness of the experience. To feel is to value the experience of the contact, and therefore what is felt is not a characteristic of the external object, but rather an activity of *nama*. Feeling is, accordingly, a mental activity. To be more precise, it is the first mental activity.

A pricked finger is painful, or to put it another way: there is a cause (the prick) and an effect (the pain). The prick is not the pain, but there is an elaboration of that contact which produces the experience of pain. Feeling, therefore, is not a quality of the object—it is not in the needle, it is not even in the flesh. Feeling is an activity of the mind. One thing is the stinging sensation; quite another, its assessment as unpleasant. We must distinguish between the perception of pain, the mental reaction of rejection, and the physical action of removing the finger, to mention just a few of the activities involved in a pricked finger. We can say that removing the finger is a reflex, even though we know that in certain circumstances we can prick ourselves without reacting (and even that there are people who prick themselves precisely to show that they "feel no pain"). Therefore the contact and activity of feeling are cause and effect, which is why we say that the experience is conditioned.

In these activities of feeling, the path of *sati* discovers the principle of everything that exists—the ontological principle that explains the nature of and relationships between being, becoming, existence, and ultimate reality. According to the law of cause and effect, there is nothing independent in the earthly, as regards *nama* or *rupa*. All physical and mental states depend on other preexisting states and arise from them, and in turn other dependent states arise when they cease. Causality is the basis of the *Dhamma*'s ontology—not a creator God, nor a universal being (*Brahman*), nor any other "transcendent creative principle." This ontological principle applies not only to matter and to the experience of matter, but also to the existence of life.

> **The interdependence between physical and mental phenomena can be understood intellectually, but for it to be effective, it has to be experienced.**

Feelings as Cognitive Activity

Matter does not feel. Feeling is a cognitive activity. Feeling is the activity that decides if the contact is favorable or unfavorable for the continuity of the organism. Feeling is the simplest cognitive activity and is vital for the three activities that allow the organism to maintain itself: nutrition, relationship, and reproduction.

An organism is matter that feels. Physical contact and the activity of feeling are the matrix on which experience is built. The sensation/feeling pairing is irreducible but identifiable from the point of view of experience.

If there is no sensation, there is no feeling—and consequently there is no experience. But sensation alone cannot keep the organism alive. The interdependence between *nama* and *rupa* is a characteristic of life. The interdependence between physical and mental phenomena can be understood intellectually, but for it to be effective, it has to be experienced.

The "I" and the "Proto-I"

The interaction between the body and the mind is mediated by an initial reaction, which is to assess the contact as pleasant, unpleasant, or neutral. From here, the mind has a second reaction and executes the behavior of drawing near, moving away, or simply not reacting. And so begins the construction of the mental construct "I." The tendency to approach or avoid foments the emergence of a repertoire of organismic behavior, which is confused with a "proto-I" whose constitutive quality is feeling—in other words, an organism that reacts to survive. Thanks to this quality, the organism learns to maintain dynamic balance, or homeostasis. Most species and living beings have evolved by following this simple pattern: open up to the nutritious or adaptive, but shut out the threatening or maladaptive.

> The Buddha discovered affective assessment to be the origin of the mind and the false idea of subjectivity.

This "proto-I" has to adapt itself to the circumstances of the environment, and to this end it uses the same affective schema. This creates a particular way of feeling the world, as well as some tendencies of action towards the felt world. It is a reactivity that adapts to the here and now, a primitive consciousness that is present in all mammals. In some species this is maintained whatever the organism's state of activation, even while asleep. The system learns and starts to create a repertoire of automatic reactions in order to be able to adapt to continuous changes in the environment.

An automated routine system which reaches a certain level of complexity needs a high-level mechanism to allow the different parts to communicate, to manage resources, and to assign control—an executive function that goes beyond the attributes of the "proto-I." However, this executive function is considered the origin of subjectivity. Because there is a felt world, there is no identity or idea of itself. Nevertheless, some neuroscientists believe they see a "nuclear self" in this executive function.

The Buddha discovered that executive function, *affective assessment*, to be the origin of the mind and the false idea of subjectivity. For some schools of thought in neuroscience, the innate responses that we share with all mammals and most other species in the animal kingdom are the first manifestations of the individual mind and the origin of the mental construct "I."

The concept "I" is just one more of the products of the conditioning that occurs over the life of an organism. It is the result of a history of reinforcement that has been neither conscious nor voluntary. As a result, "I" is the product of a series of activities, and its future is subject to that conditioning. Just because it is subject does not mean that it becomes a subject in the sense that it owns itself, but rather exactly the opposite. "I" is not a stable and permanent entity but a dependent and volatile activity. Today it would be called "liquid."

The sensation stage starts building the notions of "I" (subject) and "mine" (object), and this duality is maintained until it crystallizes completely and remains at the conceptual level. It seems to us something completely "normal" because the subject-object relationship is the basis of cognition. What begins as a complex physiological process that arose conditionally develops into a conceptualization between the subject and the object, a duality.

The Buddha himself used terms like "I," "you," "he," "she," etc., but he did so only to facilitate communication in conventional speech with conventional understanding (*paññati*). To communicate in light of absolute realities (*paramatha*) is a much more difficult challenge. Hence the Buddha does not teach destruction. Instead of teaching us to destroy the "I," he guides us to transcend the ignorance that arises from attributing a substantial reality to the "I."

The Buddha taught that individual personality is a functional integrity, unified and causally interconnected, that operates at many levels. He understood its convenient and useful functionality but viewed it as a cognitive fiction. He acknowledged the sense of individuality, of self, to be a feeling that can contract and expand according to context. There is no justification for supposing that Buddha encouraged the annihilation of this feeling of "I." Actually, the reality of all the feelings and emotions that occur in the flow of experience is relevant for an explanation of a harmonious life. So, the Buddha spoke of "I" or "myself" but avoided and discouraged "my" or "mine" because both terms imply egotism.

In fact, the "I" refers to an illusory epiphenomenon, a secondary effect or byproduct that arises from but does not causally influence a process. It is a useful abbreviation that represents a very large number of identifications, schemas, and transactions, both chemical and electrical, that occur every single second. The practice of *sati* leads to the transcendence of this concept through serenity in order to free us from the illusion of "being in control" of ourselves.

The belief in and fascination for this "I," and the useless adherence to the personal identities it brings about, are the root cause of personal and social suffering. The specific negative expressions of this ignorance at the individual level include lust, hatred, and self-deception. At a social level, some of the symptoms are fights, disputes, petty disagreements, vanity, dogma, slander, or jealousy. What the Buddha discovered upon "awaking" was that, in contrast to a static and inherent "I," there is only one phylogenetic conditioning (instinct) and another ontogenetic conditioning (habit) which become "I." Any contact leads to desire, which in turn causes attachment, and the repetition becomes "I."

Instinct and Habit

It is difficult for us to think of instinct and habit as two cognitive activities of feeling. This is because of the conceptual separation between "learned behavior" (or habit) and "biological inheritance" (or instinct). These activities dissociated due to considering "behavior" as a psychological activity unrelated to biology—or, to put it another way, due to separating the genetic components from the ethological in evolutionary processes.

We can tackle materiality from a physical or chemical perspective—approaching it analytically and separating out its primary elements, or synthetically, broadening the perspective, as with organic chemistry. For a long time, chemists thought that synthesizing organic substances required what they called "vital force," i.e., a living organism—until the barrier between organic and inorganic substances was broken "scientifically." Discovering the underlying mechanism does not stop the phenomenon from being a "mental invention"—an evolutionary solution involving matter and mind.

The difference between organic chemistry and organic biology is that genes have a history—they have been structured with the passing of time—while an organic molecule is only a witness to its present. So, in the *Dhamma*, the "vital faculty" is part of what is seen as "subtle materiality" and refers to the way in which behavior, which has arisen from mental activity in its relationship with matter, has structured the latter during the evolutionary process.

A limited view of evolution leads us to think that genes are the true evolutionary agent over and above the organism. But the simplest solution might be to think that it is the organisms, due to their actions and choices, that achieve greater representation of their genes in the following generations. Genes are the product and not the cause of evolution. This point of view became more and more accepted by scientists and evolutionists throughout the twentieth century. It is not very logical to believe in adaptation to the environment without the active component of behavior—it is like wings without flight or fins without swimming.

Today there is a certain agreement that, apart from genetics, there are other paths of transgenerational inheritance, such as *epigenetics*, which refers to the conditions that allow genes to express themselves; *the behavioral*, which refers to the inheritance of behavior patterns and is helped by learning; and finally, *the symbolic*, which is linked to language. What we call instinct is nothing magical, logical, or permanent, but rather a type of knowledge that develops in relation to the environment through learning and builds the peripheral sensory system, the regulatory systems such as the hormonal system, and patterns of connection of neuronal activity.

Additionally, animals' behavior appears to be controlled by feedback mechanisms that exercise control over the way in which behaviors occur, using the sensory information that enters the organism whilst said actions take place. Beyond learning and feedback activities, there are other cognitive and metacognitive activities that include a conscious elaboration of adaptive responses.

Consequently, to have an expanded vision of how feeling activities influence our lives, we will have to cross the conceptual border between psychological and physiological activities. We must see "instinct" as the crystallization of a "habit" and overcome the rigid dichotomy between innate and learned. Neither the fact that there is a block of reasonably stable and differentiated matter, nor that it has cognitive systems that temporarily maintain its cohesion, seems to justify the idea that "I" is the owner of the matter and the guarantor of cohesion.

Innate or Acquired

It is very hard to understand and experience pleasure and pain as mental phenomena. For humans in general, it is quite clear that the pain is in the body and that "I" cannot avoid it whenever "I" want. The experience of pleasure or pain is not a sensation, but neither is it an instinct, a reflex, or an emotion. It includes sensory information, but it is also a feeling—in other words, an assessment influenced by biographical and sociocultural conditioning. In fact, when we experience this feeling without attachment or rejection, the experience changes—it oscillates and ceases.

Not all contacts between sensory bases and receptors are pleasant or painful, although all are evaluated, and that valence is integrated into the mind's flow of feeling, or affective tone, at each moment. Pleasure and pain are a special class of feeling because of their strength, intensity, and influence over general affective tone. Pleasure and pain are sudden and brusque reactions of the mind, and they are programmed or conditioned to break into consciousness without any mediating conscious elaboration.

But it is not only pleasure and pain that are innate conditioned affective reactions. There is a whole range of feeling activities that belong to this area and interact with somatic and cognitive activities, giving rise to the pleasant and unpleasant phenomena of the experience.

Let us suppose that a person who drinks six coffees a day stops drinking altogether. Before the end of the day, they begin to get a headache and feel angry. There is no apparent sensation from external physical contact, but they nevertheless feel bodily discomfort that causes an unhealthy emotional state.

When a person loses their mobile phone, there is no contact or imbalance in the organism due to the lack of a physical element. However, they experience an anxiety attack, accompanied by various bodily aches and then dejection.

A person is told that a loved one has died, and there is a cascade of physical and mental reactions. Or, one person saves another who was about to fall off a cliff and lose their life, and both people feel great joy. Feeling can be discerned in the flow of experience, even if it cannot be extracted from that flow. Feeling is one of the activities that make up experience.

A lack of nutrients in the body is "interpreted" as being unpleasant and predisposes us towards the search for satisfaction. This predisposition is experienced as hunger—that is to say, a conditioned reaction of the organism caused by the lack of food. It cannot be said that it is a learned response, but rather an "innate affective reaction."

However, this innate affective reaction can be modified by environmental circumstances or cognitive elaborations. There is nobody who has ever decided to be hungry. Neither does the behavior of sating hunger need an "I."

External circumstances influence the development of organisms in ways that would not be appropriate to qualify as learning. There are apparently innate behaviors that do not develop until the animal is adult (such as the reproductive), while others develop from the very beginning and are improved by repetition. The discussion about behavior becomes a disquisition on whether what determines action is innate (if it originates in the nervous system) or acquired (if it comes from the environment in the form of learning or a conditioned reflex). A rigid innate-learned dichotomy cannot account for the causes of behavior that can be categorized as, for example, physiological or morphological, adaptive, evolutionary (phylogenetic), and developmental (ontogenetic).

Conditioned reflexes are those that have been produced by conditioning based on the experience of feeling, as in the case of Pavlov's famous dogs. If the dog always sees a light come on before receiving food, when the light comes on the dog will prepare to eat through a series of internal and external activities, such as salivating. The light coming on starts the activities just as seeing the food used to. One thing is the need for food, another the desire to eat, and yet another the behavior of searching for food or eating. The need for food is associated with the desire to eat, and this can be associated with an element unrelated to the food. Through conditioning, we produce behavior in the absence of the stimulus that would normally cause it.

Desire and Reaction

Desire is the lack of something and is therefore experienced as dissatisfaction or as "unpleasant." Desire sets off the search for pleasure to remedy that lack. Desire is one thing and the search for satisfaction is another. To deal with the unsatisfactory situation of desire one can avoid what is considered the source of dissatisfaction or try to find a way to alleviate the desire, even if it is partially or temporarily. This longing for satisfaction, which is mediated by materiality, is called *thana* in the *Dhamma*. It can also be generated mentally once you learn how to represent objects without the need for their material presence.

The action which seeks the solution to desire is what the *Dhamma* calls attachment (*upadana*), and it is considered to be the origin of suffering. The response to desire is what is learned (attachment), while desire (*thana*) is said to be "innate" or "natural."

This learning by conditioning is something that we share with many animal species that have desires or affects. We suffer when we do not have what we need; we also suffer by trying to avoid it being taken away when we do have it. We are programmed in a very basic way to seek what we like and reject what we do not like.

In the human being, the search for pleasure and the avoidance of pain are subject to cultural and social norms. We do not necessarily do what the body demands; rather, we weigh the consequences that our behavior will have based on what is legal or normative in our society or culture.

These norms are internalized and learned, and we respond to them in a conditioned way. This causes cognitive dissonances, which are mental conflicts caused by the appearance of a contradiction. It may be a thought that contradicts some idea, belief, or impulse, or a behavior that conflicts with learned beliefs or values. This provokes a series of internal reactions which affect the balance of the organism and constitute obstacles to mental and/or physiological health.

So, we have two forms of matter: the physical elements that are the building blocks, and the activities that, through these same elements, maintain the functioning of the organism. To explain this, we must resort to the concept of "subtle materiality" of which the *Dhamma* speaks. Here, subtle materiality refers to the physiological processes that modulate the working of the rest of the body. They are the "top-down" control systems that have become structured in matter, the tools of the mind to manage the body.

In today's times we would be talking about the nervous, endocrine, or immune systems. The *Dhamma*, on the other hand, talks about cohesion, nutrition, femininity, masculinity, vital faculty, the base of the heart, bodily intention, verbal intention, space, lightness, plasticity, spaciousness, and the stages in the life cycle of the organism. All these elements influence feelings at each moment, although they cannot be controlled except by learning from experience and practicing deconditioning.

> **Attachment is the habit of responding automatically to desire with learned behavior.**

For instance, the lack of nutrition produces the experience of hunger, which is considered an unpleasant experience. The mental state of wanting to stop this unpleasant experience is called desire. The desire to eat is momentarily satiated by food. Whenever the sensation of hunger arises, food is sought. Therefore, one thing is desire, and another is satisfaction. In terms of *Dhamma*, one thing is desire and another attachment. Attachment is the habit of responding automatically to desire with learned behavior.

The structure, therefore, is as follows: first, a physical sensation, followed by an automatic assessment as unpleasant, a desire for the sensation to disappear, a search for an object that satisfies, momentary satisfaction, repetition, habit formation, attachment to the object, identification with the attachment or clinging, and finally, the construction of character.

Deconditioning is the reverse process. It is realizing the identification, understanding the consequences of the habit, attempting to break the habit, repeatedly abstaining from reaction, experiencing dissatisfaction, finding satisfaction with the freedom of not reacting mechanically, experiencing the physical sensation as it really is, and finally, attaining freedom from the unpleasantness of the physical sensation.

Experiencing dissatisfaction is inevitable. Everybody undergoes being forgotten, ignored, or rejected. If what was previously assessed as being unpleasant can now be experienced for what it really is—whether a somatic, affective, or cognitive experience—there will be no need to defend oneself against it. See Figure 8 for an illustration of these concepts.

Here's another example: The male body is conditioned by the reproductive instinct, which causes an erection that may be painful, followed by a consequent state of actively seeking out a sexual object.

The urgency coming from the physical sensation interpreted as unpleasant is what is called desire. If each time the unpleasant sensation of desire is experienced, the response is always the same and satisfaction is obtained, even if only momentary and partial, there is a creation of an attachment—or clinging—to that activity or object through which the partial satisfaction was achieved.

Yet another example: When the body feels something unpleasant, it reacts by screaming. This would seem to be an "innate" reaction. Through shouting some of the discomfort is relieved, and this produces a type of

Contemplation of the Activities of Feeling

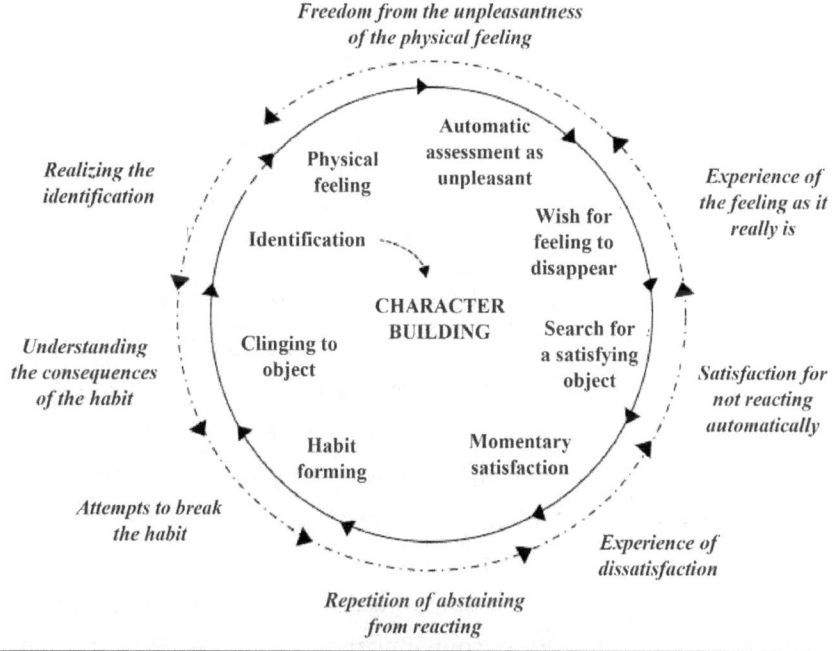

Figure 8: How character is constructed and deconstructed.

satisfaction. When another body perceives the other person's scream, it can react empathically and feel the pain of the other person. Their reaction can either be to avoid the unpleasant feeling it produces or to respond compassionately by drawing near to help.

The verbal and bodily intentions demonstrated through this gesture are reactions programmed by the body itself—part of the behaviors related to the activities of feeling. In this case the body itself, depending on the circumstances, reacts to the reaction. So, the system actually consists of two reactions.

When sati is applied to the processes of feeling, it uncovers the conditioning—the causal relationship between the first and the second reaction—between desire and attachment to what satisfies it, even if that satisfaction is only partial and momentary.

When we are hungry, we look for food. If there is no hunger, we do not look for food. The attachment reaction arises because there is desire, and desire arises from sensory impression—from the physical sensation resulting from contact between the sensory organ and the object.

In each instance there is a physical sensation, an unpleasant feeling, and organismic reaction. We could call one phase passive or innate, and another active or learned, although the terms "innate" and "learned" lose meaning when there is deep contemplation.

Back to the *Sutta*: The Mind-Body Connection

Three complete versions of the *Satipatthāna Sutta* exist—one in Pali and two in Chinese. There is a fourth incomplete version in Sanskrit in the *Prajnaparamita Sutra*. While the latter does not include the discrimination between the first three foundations, and therefore contains no section dedicated to feelings, the other three diverge as regards the approach to the second foundation of attention. The translations also vary.

All three speak of three feelings—pleasant, unpleasant, and neutral—but differ in relation to areas of contemplation. The translation of the *Sutta* that we have chosen speaks of "worldly" and "spiritual." In the others, "bodily," "mental," "sensual," and "not sensual" are added, and in one it is specified that there can be no mixed feelings—if there is a pleasant feeling, there can be no unpleasant feeling, and vice versa.

These differences and this ambiguity regarding the activities of feeling are due to their dual material and mental aspect. Depending on the perspective taken, the pain is either in the body or in the mind. As we do not like this type of ambiguity, we tend to choose one explanation and reject the other. The tradition of Western thinking tends towards the assumption that there is an external reality that is the cause, and science, consequently, has sought the solution to suffering in the exterior.

So, as we have discussed in some previous examples, a sensation may be the product of contact between a mental object and the mental receptor, and there would still be a physical correlate. As we will see later, the *Dhamma* speaks of six senses, as it considers the intellect to be another sense.

In any case, there is no activity in the mind without activity in the body, nor activity in the body without activity in the mind, from the point of view of experience. The mind is in the body and the body is in the mind. This is the understanding of *namarupa*, according to the Buddha's method.

Evidently, the body functions because it is not an isolated organism. There is a continuous interaction with its environment and among its own components (nutrition, relationship, and reproduction)—it is dependent on the food the body gets from the environment, as well as on the relationships established with other beings, and therefore is impermanent. Each contact it performs is elaborated cognitively as pleasant, unpleasant, or neutral, which means that dissatisfaction is part of being. If nobody would wish for this to be different from how it is, then nobody would suffer.

Once again, be wary of the temptation to reduce the scope of experience to the physiological or neurological substrate. Contemplation of somatic activities leads us to the understanding that all experience involves matter and what one realizes about matter. What is realized about matter cannot be separated from matter itself, and you cannot know if there is matter without the realization.

This does not presuppose a dualistic conception, viewing the mind and body as two different substances, given that it does not imply a subject and an object. As we have already said, Buddha proposes a method based on direct experience. In this sense, you could say that the mind is the forerunner, as it is the mind that realizes that there is a body, feelings, or thoughts. The *Dhamma* does not carry out the operation of realizing that there is matter and then pretend that the realizing comes from matter, as materialistic metaphysics does. It starts from the basis of the only thing that is certain, that there is consciousness of matter.

The fact that there are some receptors (including the brain) that capture their objects implies that there is contact between them and that there is an organismic interpretation of the contact that we call mind. However, this is not an "I" (or, in philosophical terms, a subject that relates them). It is another type of substance, which is precisely what a

Integral Vipassana

dualism would imply. In any case, the Buddha avoided this type of speculation because it is outside of the experience.

Science wants to carry out this subtraction operation of the subject by reducing it to its material components. The latest explanation is that of a physiological change—a reduction of experience to electrical and chemical interactions.

As we have already stated, this is not the Buddha's method. The functioning of the amygdala or limbic system cannot explain the complex network of values, beliefs, expectations, dependencies, emotional habits, contextual or situational aspects, and other factors that underlie a feeling or an emotional reaction. The scientific method is just one more way to acquire knowledge—one which has led to many benefits and improvements for humanity. However, it is no use in explaining the processes that have conditioned the emergence of the enormous diversity of species and individuals on the planet. Arguably, these processes are none other than feeling activities—even to the extent that they have driven natural selection throughout history.

As we have seen, an organism perceives each of the many millions of contacts it makes at each and every moment. Perception arises from the feeling—either pleasant, unpleasant, or neutral in every contact—creating an apparent continuity. Therefore, we can continually experience feeling if we turn our attention towards that register of experience. The experience is pleasant, unpleasant, or neutral at all times. Contemplation of feeling reveals causality and its consequence—*conditioning*. When we contemplate the pleasant, unpleasant, or neutral aspect of the experience, we tend to cling to the pleasant and avoid the unpleasant. Clinging, therefore, is a reaction to the feeling.

The translation of the *Sutta* speaks of "carnal sensations" and "spiritual sensations." According to our interpretation, this refers to activities of feeling, or feelings. Contemplation "in" the experience has led us to the recognition that there cannot be mental activity without physical activity. Therefore, the reference to carnal and spiritual is a necessary discrimination, but one that needs an explanation.

The text makes sense if we interpret that there are feelings that arise directly from somatic activities—in other words, from the contact between matter and mind—and others that do not require contact with matter. Although the translation does not differentiate between pleasure/pain and pleasant/unpleasant, in other traditional texts the former dichotomy is limited to the body and the latter is reserved for the mental experience. Pleasure and pain are the way to feel the body, whereas pleasant and unpleasant are the way to feel the activity of the mind. There are physical experiences of pleasure and pain, and pleasant or unpleasant mental experiences. The body has its special way of feeling, and the mind also has its own. In this sense it could be said that one thing is the sensory feeling and another the spiritual feeling. Strictly speaking, both are mental experiences, but the former arise from physical contact and the latter do not.

Affective Valence

Additionally, in the *Sutta*, contemplation of the activities of feeling is directed towards experiencing the "affective valence," which discriminates between pleasant, painful, or indifferent feelings. In fact, in this ambit of affective consciousness it is more accurate to talk about when something is *activated or not* than about innate and learned reactions, or conscious and unconscious.

In the *Sutta* we are not urged to reject the unpleasant and cling to the pleasant, but rather to recognize the change in affective tone at every moment. The rejection of the unpleasant and the yearning for the pleasant are the root of dissatisfaction. When we react to the pleasant or unpleasant, we reinforce the connections that link affective reactions, whereas when we do not react, we weaken them.

> **The rejection of the unpleasant and the yearning for the pleasant are the root of dissatisfaction.**

There are homeostatic affects (such as hunger or thirst), sensory affections that arise from contact between the object and the receptor, and primary emotional affects (or reflexes). There are feelings that have been learned through sensitization, habituation, and conditioning. There are systems for affective regulation, and there are intentions that include reflection, planning, and the execution of emotions.

In the Buddha's *Dhamma*, which is a profound contemplation on the process of experience, this differentiation is fundamental. It is a highly liberating insight because, when it is understood that sensations always arise associated with desire, which is then followed by an emotional habit, one can learn not to react to desire in a way that produces unhealthy consequences. Reacting is an attempt to fulfill the desire through a habit, but as each contact stimulates desire, we spend our lives trying to fulfill desires without realizing that this is not the solution to dissatisfaction. After all, the very next contact will cause a new desire.

Desire represents existential dissatisfaction and must be understood and accepted. There is nothing that can satisfy desire permanently because it is coded into bodily material and is its "default" way of functioning.

The contacts between an object and receiver sensor are categorized as being desirable, undesirable, or indifferent, and the automatic response is to retain the desirable, avoid the undesirable, and ignore the indifferent. One thing is the physical sensation associated with mental valence, but quite another the action taken in response. Understanding this mechanism may eventually free us from affective and cognitive aspects that influence malaise.

On the other hand, feeling is a primary mental activity or a secondary conditioned response, while emotion is a third-degree activity that includes internal elaboration and its external manifestation. Emotion is both internal and external. On many occasions, it is released without us recognizing the feeling. This is why what is known as "emotional intelligence" is so important—it attempts to teach us how to recognize feelings so as to allow them to be expressed, emotionally or not.

Many primary feelings and secondary affective reactions are involuntary and automatic. As regards primary feelings or secondary conditioning, human beings can come up with answers that break rigid and instinctive schemas or those conditioned by learning. The elaborated response, observable internally or externally, is emotion.

Emotion is a "top-down" activity and, therefore, belongs to the third foundation of attention. Feelings arise from primary reflexes, from instinctive reactions, and from conditioning by consequences. They are not intentional or planned activities, but rather flow from the depths of our psyche or are a product of affective reactivity. These activities can be examined through the cultivation of *sati*.

Cause and Effect: Material and Mental Phenomena

The profound vision of Vipassana begins with the understanding that there are material phenomena and mental phenomena. We understand that air and the nose on which it impacts are both matter, while the tactile sensation and *what causes* the tactile sensation is mind. We understand that something impacts on the ear, and that both things are matter (sound, for example, being a wave that can be measured and located in time and space), but auditory awareness is mind.

> **Experience is no more than a dizzying activity of interaction between physical and mental phenomena.**

We understand that the body is matter, and that the body is what actually is sitting, but the mind is what realizes you have sat down. There is nothing but matter and mind interacting.

Remember that we are exploring experience. We do not take for granted the existence of an external reality. The only reality is the experience of each moment, and experience is no more than a dizzying activity of interaction between physical and mental phenomena.

Attentive observation of experience shows that sometimes matter is the cause and mind is the effect, while at other times mind is the cause and matter is the effect. For instance, air in contact with the nose is the cause, and tactile awareness is the effect. However, the decision to stand up is the cause of the body standing up, while the upright body is the effect. Thus, existence is nothing more than the cause-effect relationship between matter and mind, and experience is its result.

The mind becomes a precursor when it acts by searching for something or avoiding something material—it approaches or recedes. For this to happen, the physical sensation must cause a reaction in the mind. If the mind did not react, there would be nothing but physical sensations, and consequently the mind would not exert any influence over the body.

In the context of evolution, affective reaction was an adaptive activity. If the object provides something necessary for survival or reproduction, it is categorized as being pleasant and leads to a predisposition to staying in touch. If it is categorized as being unpleasant, the opposite happens, and if it is categorized as neutral it does not predispose towards anything.

The assessment guides the organism depending on the strength of contact. The fact that there is a third category, neutral, demonstrates that for a stimulus to be able to exercise this guiding function in the body, the mind, or the organism, it must exceed a certain threshold. Below this threshold, the stimulus goes unnoticed. It is not always the case that the same stimulus has the same adaptive value for survival or reproduction, nor even the same force when it appears, hence the organism has to learn to manage the mental skill to guide its attention and to select stimuli from among all the incoming information. The reward or frustration experienced as a result of the reaction generates the learning. The repetition of a sequence of contact, desire, reaction, and reward establishes a habit.

Desire will not stop appearing because the organism needs to evaluate all contacts in order to know their adaptive value and elicit a response. Nevertheless, the reaction is what may be healthy or unhealthy—and this is what ultimately reproduces the discomfort. One thing is desire and another the reaction in the shape of attachment to its palliative. When the reaction is repeated and learned, it turns into clinging. The self becomes accustomed to interpreting that reaction as being part of itself: "I am like that," "It is so," "I like it or I don't like it."

The evaluation is carried out in the six sensory spheres as defined in *Dhamma* psychology: sight, hearing, touch, smell, taste, and intellect. The intellect, or cognitive sense, is a sixth sense that has its sensory base in the heart, and its sensory objects are the mental representations. Each sensory base receives the object to which it is sensitive and out of this contact arises the awareness of each sense. The immediate function of this system is to decide if the object is dangerous or beneficial. For example, let us imagine something solid impacting the body and producing tactile awareness. This awareness assesses whether the contact is pleasant, unpleasant, or neutral, depending on the intensity and other contextual characteristics beyond what has already been learned from previous contacts. This information will be combined with the reference to many other contacts to produce a perception of the situation. This perception triggers a mental reaction, which may lead to bodily activity.

As we have seen, there are different levels in the activities of feeling. On the one hand we have innate, biologically determined behavior patterns, and on the other hand we have reflexes or involuntary and automatic responses to certain stimuli. A repertoire of learned responses is built up based on these fixed and reflex reactions, some of which are highly complex, as well as on those activities that we call reflexive, such as thinking, planning, and higher forms of intentionality.

The first are called "intentions in action" (*Panksepp*), because despite being involuntary, they have an intention, adaptation, or survival. The second are called conditioned or learned, as they are the result of learning. The third are called "intentions of action," or motivations, because they respond to a plan or consciously seek an objective and belong to the third foundation of attention.

So, what we call feelings is actually a complex construction that began in very ancient phases of the evolutionary process and then crystallized into an implicit programming that we call instinctive reaction, or reflex.

Reflexes and Conditioning

There are many types of reflexes and automatic reactions. Some begin at the moment of birth and others are learned during the first years of life. While "reflex acts" are said to be innate, genetic, or the products of evolution, "conditioned responses" develop throughout the whole life of the organism as it acquires new experiences.

There are archaic reflexes, such as sucking or grip, and vegetative reflexes which deal with homeostasis or vegetative balance of the organism. These are managed by different levels of the spinal cord, such as those that produce penile erection, dilation of the vagina, ejaculation, sweat secretion, etc. Some are organized in the spinal bulb (medulla oblongata), a thickening of the medulla near to the brain, and they control breathing, circulation, or swallowing. The vegetative functioning of the body is regulated and controlled by reflexes.

Nevertheless, a conditioned reflex is a learned response. A stimulus that was previously considered indifferent becomes the originator of an automatic response. For instance, the sucking reflex is triggered when a bib is placed on the baby—it is not necessary to physically stimulate the baby's mouth. The new response to putting on the bib is an example of conditioned reflex, which is not innate but rather acquired.

A reflex act is an action performed by a set of anatomical structures as a stereotyped and *involuntary response to a specific stimulus*. But it is important to distinguish this from the popular use of the word "reflex" to refer to complex movements that are rapid. The correct term to refer to this type of movement is "ballistic movements," which are carried out very quickly but require prior conscious learning, as well as improvement through practice, such as when we drop something and manage to catch it before it falls to the ground. It is not a reflex because it requires the coordination of numerous motor areas of the cerebral cortex, which does not intervene in reflexes that are processed subcortically.

To construct response patterns of this type, other types of activities are required, such as reasoning strategies that can distance themselves from the present situation to foresee happenings or to make plans. In other words, they need an expansion of awareness involving the experience of the past and anticipation of the future. They also require a biographical memory and an organismic consciousness.

What is important in all these types of behavior is that they are based on the affective scheme of reacting to the pleasant, the unpleasant, or the neutral. This may be conscious to a greater or lesser degree, but either way most of our repertoire of internal and external behaviors are conditioned by the affective schema.

However, there is more than classical conditioning or conscious learning. Nowadays we know that a large part of everyday reactions has been conditioned by their consequences—that is to say, if one gets good consequences, the action tends to be repeated, but if they turn out negative, they tend not to be repeated. It is our basic way of learning. Operant conditioning, or learning by consequences, develops new behaviors through positive or negative reinforcement of a response. Reward or punishment is the basic schema of emotional life.

Another type of conditioning, *evaluative conditioning*, allows a neutral stimulus, associated by space-time contiguity with a pleasant stimulus, to be experienced as pleasant. The same goes for unpleasant stimuli. This type of conditioning also does not need to be "perceived" to be established—it is installed subliminally, and is thus very difficult to extinguish or decondition. If it is the case that operant conditioning develops new behaviors to adapt to the environment, evaluative conditioning develops the preferences of the individual. It is quite understandable that we find it so difficult to modify our habits because, in many cases, we are not aware of how they came about or of the stimuli that set them off.

So far, humankind has discovered other types of conditioning that do not need conscious processing. These include "priming," where if a stimulus is presented, the chances of that stimulus being chosen at a later date are increased. Another example is the memory of patterns, which explains how we apply rules that we are unaware of in order to carry out complex actions, such as ballistic movements, a skill that we share with other animals like rats. This is how we learn many social norms, or language.

The important point is that we learn without needing to be aware of it. We associate a stimulus with a feeling, a feeling with an action, a feeling with a desire, a feeling with another feeling—all in a totally involuntary way that's driven by the simple hedonic "load" of stimuli, feelings, or actions. This affective programming can even make us deflect a feeling before we know that we have it.

This is all extremely important because it means that a great deal of our behavior and of our emotional life happens without us understanding exactly why it happens. For instance, when we are driven by the avoidance of displeasure, or when we exhibit poor adaptive behaviors to achieve adaptive objectives, we create a poor adaptive response pattern. Sometimes, we behave to avoid displeasure in a way that generates response patterns which, paradoxically, are not adaptive. Other times we carry out apparently unadaptive behaviors that, nevertheless, produce adaptive effects.

It seems that the very continuity of the idea of "I" may be the product of this affective but non-conscious learning. All this has limited the expectations of psychotherapy, since if something is recorded emotionally, we might be able to learn to regulate its triggering, but we may never be able to completely eliminate the automatic response. *Sati* (mindfulness) has had quite good results in this regard.

So, the affective patterns composed of reactions on which our mental life appears to be constructed are shaped by reinforcements and punishments. They turn into learned reactions that remain transparent to consciousness and are triggered without the need for conscious mediation.

We have blocks of automated activity that interrelate through multiple connections to form networks. These blocks only exist when activated, and when not activated they only exist as a possibility. The connections can be activators or inhibitors, and their value is the strength of connection. Nobody manages these processes consciously—they are impersonal and unstoppable, continuously searching for a satisfaction that never arrives because they themselves are their only reason to exist. Despite our belief that we are reasonable and free beings, we actually are more reactive than we would like to believe.

The presence of *sati* reveals the reactivity. *Sati* enters into processes that were hidden from consciousness and allows us to see the causal links that lead to learning and conditioning. The "vision" that *sati* provides can help change the tendency towards conditioning and lead to its ultimate extinction. Conscious attention is a requirement for release from the emotional bonds that control most behavior.

We share with many other beings the search for survival resources, but this very search has become a compulsion. Because there is desire, we generate certain response patterns, repeating and clinging to a series of mental reactions and physical behaviors. These reactions eventually form a fictional character ("I am eating," "I am Red (Manchester United)," "I am a philosopher"). When we place this character on a pedestal as the most important in the world, suffering is guaranteed because, obviously, this character is *not* the most important thing for the world. The "I" bases its happiness on the world fulfilling its desires and expectations, but the world just continues on its own course.

> **Conscious attention is a requirement for release from the emotional bonds that control most behavior.**

Feelings: The Key to the Whole Process

The paragraph in the *Sutta* dedicated to feelings is short, but it is key to the whole process. If you are able to discriminate between physical phenomena and mental phenomena, you discover that pleasure and pain are simple physical sensations, and what makes them pleasant or unpleasant is mental assessment. However, if you can manage to differentiate the pleasure and the pain that depend on the body from the pleasant and unpleasant that do *not* depend on the body, then you can access a mental place where affective programming is able to transcend dependence on the body. This is what is called "spiritual sensation" in the *Sutta* and what we would describe in our commentary as "mental feeling."

For example, in a meditation, you may be experiencing bodily discomfort due to immobility and at the same time, but with greater intensity, be rejoicing in the stability of the mind or in the pleasure of its serenity.

In more technical terms, the pleasurable feeling characteristic of the first *jhana*, or deep state, of Vipassana is not caused by the search for sensual pleasure, in the same way that the equanimity of the fourth *jhana* of Vipassana is not caused by ignorance due to a neutral sensual feeling.

When we recognize in ourselves the effects of feelings—in other words, how they cause unconscious actions and reactions, how willpower alone is insufficient to control them because they are coded into biological programming, and how they traverse all levels of the psyche from the most primary and animal up to the most elaborate forms of thought and rationality—then we become extremely aware of our vulnerability and lack of control. This understanding of our limitations makes us develop an attitude of kindness not only toward ourselves, but also to others as we understand that they are in the same situation as us.

That also then extends toward all forms of life that function through feelings and the affective assessment of contacts with the outer world.

This attitude of kindness becomes happiness when we see others in a positive emotional state, and compassion when we see them in a negative state. Caring for others, together with caring for oneself—both of which are part of these primary emotional forces—surfaces from the labyrinth of conditioning and presents the true facet of those animals that care for their young, and in so doing learn to care for the species. The feelings of care are the basis of love and also belong to that biological bedrock whence conscious activity arises. One learns to fight for survival, but also to *care* for survival.

We sometimes refer to feelings as if they were more human than reasoning, but in reality feelings are more instinctive and less evolved than mental values. Feelings are subject to biological imperatives, while rationality implies seeing the other as "another like me."

Feeling and reasoning do not mutually contradict. In fact, rationality arises as a way of escaping, at least partially, the determination of affective impulses. Thanks to rationality we understand that if the only value is welfare of the self, then the result would be the rule of the strongest, and we would be in a state of permanent war with each other. Social and cultural values aim to transcend instinctive conditioning and represent aspects of the common good. This transcendence of basic instinct is what is referred to in the *Sutta* as "spiritual sensation."

Immeasurable Affective States

When we know our biological impulses inside and out, we can develop states of mind free from needs, preferences, or physiological and personal interests. In Buddha's tradition they are called *immeasurable states of mind*—such as goodness, joy, or compassion—which, being unbalanced and biased towards the pleasant, are not limited to the personal, but rather more widely focused on universal well-being. They are the highest states of the activities of feeling. Given that they are mental states and not only affective tendencies or feelings, they actually belong to the third foundation of attention, but they can also be seen as "spiritual emotions" for their self-transcendent and universal character.

The practice of conscious attention therefore clearly affects our understanding of how feelings work, and it also affects emotional regulation. This effect has been found in research into modern mindfulness, leading to a current of opinion which has set compassion as the main objective of that practice.

Compassion, nevertheless, would be the mature fruit of contemplating feelings. This contemplation first leads to becoming aware of how one treats oneself and then to the comprehension of the emotional advantages of treating oneself well.

By learning to be kind to yourself, it becomes easier to be happy when you see others in a good emotional state because you realize their wellbeing results in your own well-being. Understanding suffering predisposes you, in the best-case scenario, to feel empowered to risk your well-being and enter into the negative emotional state of another person. This action, which is called compassion, is a risky activity which should never be undertaken by anybody who is not sure that they will not be overwhelmed by the negative state of the other person. Furthermore, such a mediation must achieve well-being for yourself and for the other person. It must not be limited to satisfying a specific demand; rather, it should help you come to some understanding about how suffering occurs.

The state that's free from the forces of attraction and rejection is known as *equanimity*, and is the most balanced and highly evolved state of feeling. Buddha's aspiration was that the cultivation of *sati* would lead as many people as possible to this state of equanimity. There are even deeper states to encounter on the path of *Nibbana*, but developing equanimity would ensure the disappearance of the vast majority of human conflicts.

In Summary

Meditation in the second foundation of attention reveals that what we call the mind begins by the introduction of a value criterion in each contact that occurs between external materiality and organismic materiality, between the object and the sensory receptor. The value is the desirability, undesirability, or indifference of the contact.

This evaluation is followed by a reaction of attachment, aversion, or ignoring that tends to repeat and so ends up being learned and then started back up automatically. While the first evaluation is a mechanism whose origin goes back to the phylogenetic scale, much of the reaction is learned during the upbringing and development of the individual—that is to say, it is ontogenetic.

Understanding the interplay of desire and attachment leads to an understanding of causation. Any physical or mental action has its effects. Action is cause and produces consequences. It is not a linear causality but rather the final cause, so in many cases the consequences of the actions are not immediate.

The affective mechanism includes all *namarupa* relationships, but it can transcend them and free the affective experience from its corporal anchorage, thereby generating mental states filled with affection that in the *Sutta* are called "pleasurable and painful spiritual sensations."

The conclusion is that we humans learn thanks to feelings, but that feelings are not "I," and that suffering is reacting to the primary feelings by ignoring them, wishing to control them, or wanting to avoid them.

3

CONTEMPLATION OF ACTIVITIES OF KNOWING

"The end of the world can never be reached by walking. However, without having reached the world's end there is no release from suffering. I declare that it is in this fathom-long carcass, with its perceptions and thoughts, that there is the world, the origin of the world, the cessation of the world, and the path leading to the cessation of the world."
(Anguttara Nikaya 4:45)

The knowing activities are the most evolved and the most complex. Their function is to coordinate the other activities.

The meditator encounters discursive thoughts known as the "narrative I" and, in principle, is convinced that these thoughts are "I." However, language is the product of a long and complex process of abstraction through which sensory data is converted into mental representations. These, in turn, are encoded in signs, symbols, and concepts with which language is constructed. The meditator only "hears" the language and believes that it faithfully represents external reality. Thus, this abstract world replaces the sensory world.

Meditators start to realize that thoughts occur spontaneously, without intervention. They think things, even though they have not decided to think them. This understanding leads them to disidentify from thoughts, to distance themselves from them, to turn them into objects. They go from believing that they themselves are the thoughts to believing that they have thoughts.

By disidentifying themselves—by turning what was thought to be a subject into an object—they can "operate" upon these thoughts. The meditator can become aware of when they appear, when they are produced, when they are the product of thinking, and when they are not the product of thinking, as well as when there are thoughts and when there are not thoughts.

Understanding Thoughts with the *Abhidhamma*

The knowing activities are the most difficult to understand in the *Dhamma*. They were not systematically explained in the *suttas*, and so to explain them, the third of the Tipitaka baskets, the *Abhidhamma*, was constructed.

The *Abhidhamma* is a detailed model of how the mind works. It is normally only accessible to monks, academics, or people solely dedicated to the study of the *Dhamma*. In this chapter we have produced as clearly as possible a summary exposition of the psychology of the *Abhidhamma*.

> **The self is not a distinct substance, a soul, or something eternal, but rather a series of interdependent activities that produce the effect—or illusion—that there is someone in control of the process.**

The key element of the activities of knowing is *citta*, which is a discrete moment of knowledge—in other words, a piece of data that arises from a contact between one of the six sensory bases and the six types of objects. As will be seen in the text, each piece of data includes the activities of knowing that we call basic psychological processes.

As they are activities that take place in the very background of the experience, only perseverant and deep meditation can make them "visible." This process of drawing back the curtains on cognitive activity converts what was a subject into an object. In other words, what was previously an implicit activity carried out by the supposed subject that knows begins to change into an activity that can be "observed." It is the process of deconstruction of the self, which makes us understand that radical Buddhist idea of the non-substantiality of the self. This notion clarifies that the self is not a distinct substance, a soul, or something eternal, but rather a series of interdependent activities that produce the effect—or illusion—that there is someone in control of the process.

Included in the knowing activities are what Western psychology calls emotions. As in psychology, the *Dhamma* also views emotions as mental artifices arising from physiological responses conditioned by the survival principle but guided by the pleasure principle. In that sense, they are "forms" in the mind that have been conditioned by the entire history of reinforcements and contingencies of the biography of the organism's mind and body.

Knowing

When contemplating the third foundation of attention, the meditator directs attention towards the "knowing activities." When this happens, what becomes most evident is internal discourse with thoughts, concepts, ideas, symbols, or images.

The "somatic activities" and the "feeling activities" are both included in those of knowing. Sensations and feelings are necessary for there to be cognitions.

The meditator understands that there is *perception* and discovers that it is the result of the integration of sensations and feelings with memories and past experiences. That understanding then leads to a realization that there is an activity of knowing or awareness of things that is mediated by mental patterns that "color" it. To sum up, that mental experience is the result of learning combined with the biographical, contextual, and socio-cultural conditioning of the psychophysical organism (body/mind).

The *Sutta* discusses being aware of states of mind "qualified" by feelings, as well as being aware of abstract mental configurations such as an "open mind," "infinite mind," "empty mind," or "free mind."

The *Abhidhamma*, which is the theoretical model of mental process that the *Dhamma* tradition has constructed through systematic observation of "knowing activities," suggests that experience is the breakneck succession of "mental moments," or *cittas*. Each *citta* needs various activities that configure it, or mental factors (*cetasikas*). Some are vital for the correct functioning of the activity of knowing, and others determine it affectively.

Conscious attention to the "knowing activities" reveals many activities through which the phenomenological experience or first-person experience is constructed. Also made conscious are many activities considered subjective, such as whether we are concentrating or not, angry or not, motivated or not, attentive or not. We realize that there is perception and that we can be aware of perception—indeed, we can be aware of any state of mind, however subtle it may be. *Sati* discloses any possible activity, voluntary or involuntary, top-down or bottom-up. The development of *sati* allows us to discover that the activity of knowing is divided into the knower and the known. This understanding leads to liberation from dissatisfaction since there is no subject who suffers—just the simple activity of knowing.

Buddha's *Dhamma* employs a specialized language for everything related to experience, precisely because that is his field of investigation. When there is a mention of "contemplation of the mind" in the translations of the *Sutta*, we have to specify what the word "mind" refers to.

The discovery that mind and matter (*namarupa*) are two necessary aspects for experience to arise leads to the understanding that the mind (*nama*) is an activity that depends on each contact with matter (*rupa*). In fact, cognitive activity begins as a simple learning mechanism.

By discriminating feelings (*nama*) from matter (*rupa*), as occurred in the second foundation of attention, mental space is opened. The mind's awareness allows for learning how to use conditioning, not just in the contacts between *nama* and *rupa* but also within *nama* activity.

Sensual pleasure can be separated from mental or spiritual pleasure. This produces a repertoire of responses which, following the same procedure, search for mental pleasure and also reject mental pain. Pleasant, unpleasant, and indifferent are mental categories on which the conventional world is built, including the idea of "I."

The reactions and responses to these categories have constructed the world that we call "real." There is nothing but matter and that which realizes matter. These have shaped a biological organism, which has created patterns and habits of interpretation and response to the contacts made by the senses, as well as to the contacts that the mind makes with its own phenomena. This not only does not detract whatsoever from the dignity of human beings but also confers dignity on the rest of sentient beings.

Satipatthāna Sutta: Contemplation of Consciousness

And how, monks, does a monk live contemplating consciousness in consciousness?

Herein, monks, a monk knows the consciousness with lust, as with lust; the consciousness without lust, as without lust; the consciousness with hate, as with hate; the consciousness without hate, as without hate; the consciousness with ignorance, as with ignorance; the consciousness without ignorance, as without ignorance; the shrunken state of consciousness, as the shrunken state; the distracted state of consciousness, as the distracted state; the developed state of consciousness, as the developed state; the undeveloped state of consciousness as the undeveloped state; the state of consciousness with some other mental state superior to it, as the state with something mentally higher; the state of consciousness with no other mental state superior to it, as the state with nothing mentally higher; the concentrated state of consciousness, as the concentrated state; the unconcentrated state of consciousness, as the unconcentrated state; the freed state of consciousness, as the freed state; and the unfreed state of consciousness, as the unfreed state.

Thus he lives contemplating consciousness in consciousness internally, or he lives contemplating consciousness in consciousness externally, or he lives contemplating consciousness in consciousness internally and externally. He lives contemplating origination factors in consciousness, or he lives contemplating dissolution-factors in consciousness, or he lives contemplating origination-and-dissolution factors in consciousness. Or his mindfulness is established with the thought, "Consciousness exists," to the extent necessary just for knowledge and mindfulness, and he lives detached, and clings to nothing in the world. Thus, monks, a monk lives contemplating consciousness in consciousness.

Citta and Its Activities

The Third Foundation of Attention is contemplation of the knowing processes (*citta*). This includes all that has access to consciousness—somatic, affective, subjective, or phenomenological awareness, whether mental or cognitive. The contemplation of the mind can be hard to understand because the subjective consciousness with which the "I" identifies—that flux of mental phenomena that we may believe to be "I"—is just one part of the activity of knowing. In other words, that subjectivity can be known, and what is believed to be subject can become object.

This third foundation of attention integrates physical experience and affective experience into the subjective mental experience, which can be observed externally as an objective mental experience. All this activity occurs based on miniature mental processes, or *cittas*, which process all these data at high speed. It includes both the somatic and the affective experience, which are cognitive processes. Each physical sense and every affective assessment function at a certain speed, or have their own cycles, and all this information has to be integrated in a coherent fashion. This is the subjective mental experience, also known as mental phenomena or *dhammas*.

Subjective mental experience can be known. The contemplation of mental phenomena allows us to recognize perception, attachment, envy, flexibility, and many other qualities which make up that subjective experience. In other words, it is possible to have an objective mental experience of the subjective experience.

Contemplation of Activities of Knowing

What Buddha came to understand is that in the cognitive process, the five sensory consciousnesses, mental awareness, mental phenomena, and the awareness of these mental phenomena all coalesce. The eye is the sensory gateway to the visible object, and its contact produces visual awareness (*cakkuviññana*) and so generates a visual sensation. Similarly, the intellect (*mano*) is the mental activity through which the object or mental phenomenon (*dhamma*) and mental consciousness (*viññana*) produce mental sensation. The eye makes contact with the shape or color which are its objects, which in turn alerts the visual awareness for visual sensation to occur. The intellect (*mano*) encounters mental phenomena (*dhammas*), which are the object of the fourth foundation of attention, and this awakens mind consciousness (*manoviññana*). Both mental phenomena (*dhammas*) and the perception of mental phenomena are *citta* activities.

Actually, all phenomena are mental since, as soon as the contact happens (or even before), the knowing activities begin—and these are mental activities. For us to realize that a physical phenomenon has occurred, it must be mentally processed. When we see a horse, for instance, it accesses our consciousness through sight as shape and color, and these, supported by other mental activities, turn it into a mental image loaded with personal meaning, which is a *dhamma*.

To see a horse, many cognitive activities (*cittas*) are needed. This *dhamma* can pass through consciousness without leaving a trace, or it can be understood as "I am seeing a horse," or "I am imagining a horse" should the horse no longer be present. In both cases it is the *citta* activity, or the *citta* process, that makes the phenomenon possible, as well as our knowledge of it.

It seems that Buddha realized that the mind is not only capable of making contact with matter and having physical sensations, but that it can also do it with its own mental activities—i.e., have mental sensations. When the mental base makes contact with a mental object (*dhamma*), this results in a mental sensation arising. The Buddha discovered that the basis, or organ, of cognitive activity is the heart.

We have already seen that the so-called "subtle materiality" controls that part of feelings that is already structured in the organism as matter. By "subtle materiality," Buddhist teaching is referring to the physiological processes that underlie how the body works. In *Dhamma* the basis of the mind (for us, the knowing activities) is the heart, and so the heart serves as the connection between *nama* and *rupa*, between somatic, affective, and cognitive activities.

Citta as the Building Block of Awareness

All this building activity of the mind/body is performed through cognition (*citta*) and cognitive patterns or basic psychological processes (*cetasikas*) that carry out the activity of knowing or being aware of something. *Citta* is the minimum unit of awareness, something like the nucleus of a cell of consciousness, and *cetasikas* are its organelles.

These mental patterns are limited to a certain number that varies depending on the different Buddhist traditions. Still, it is a pedagogical approach that tries to be as accurate as possible without falling into dogmatism. As it is with the attention system (*sati, samadhi, vayama*), the conventional scale used to observe experience does not permit us to understand the activity of *citta*. This arises and ceases in each of the innumerable contacts between materiality and mind, as well as between the mind itself and what the mind realizes.

The enormous speed at which the *cittas* arise and cease has led to the "parallel processing" to which we referred in this book's Introduction. The *cittas* are compacted into information blocks that function as a unit to give a faster and consequently more adaptive response, useful in situations like imminent danger. We are used to processing information through these *paññatti*, or compound phenomena, which by becoming automatic turn into realities and set off conditioned response patterns (*sankharas*). Later, these realities constructed by the mind/body are given a name or a designation. And this is how mental representations are generated.

Representations are abstractions made out of the interplay between *nama* and *rupa*. They are "castles in the air," constructed from the sensations we collect from the six senses (including cognitive activity as a sixth sense). This process of "conceptualization" (*paññati*) of reality, crystallized in language, becomes "the truth" through which we interpret experience. This is the origin of the imaginary world, fantasies, planning, beliefs, expectations, and philosophies—all conceptual systems that help us to interpret reality.

> **The practice of sati aims to purify all unconscious conditioning.**

This conceptualized way of living can be conscious or unconscious. Unconscious cognitive processes rule a great deal of our internal and external behavior, thereby generating more conditioning, greater inertia, and less awareness of the ultimate realities they are built upon.

The practice of *sati* aims to purify all unconscious conditioning. In this context the term "unconscious" refers to mental activity that is not detected in the experience, but can be recognized by its results.

We must remember that the Buddha's method does not take external reality for granted, but rather is only interested in *the current experience in progress*, while the conventional view is that the only reality is that which the senses detect.

Citta and the Seven Mental Processes

When *Citta* arises, it is always accompanied by at least seven mental processes (*cetasikas*)—contact, feeling, perception, intention, focus, mental vitality, and attention. As there can be no cognitive process without them, they are deemed universal. Through them all objects are known. If one is not dead, in a coma, or in deep sleep, cognitive activity requires these processes. Thus, even when daydreaming, we do several things at once. Or if we think in a completely unstructured way, these factors always co-operate to help guide and support cognitive activity (*citta*) in knowing an object. At each moment these seven factors work together to build meaning out of the incoming torrent of stimuli.

It may seem that we are deliberately choosing to shift our attention from one object to another, but most of the time our behavior is controlled by the conditioning of these factors, which are completely beyond our conscious attention. Paradoxically, even though *citta*, cognitive activity, and the universal *cetasikas* (basic cognitive processes) are always present, we can be completely unaware of them.

When we realize that there really *are* universal processes, and we start to consciously work on them, other processes come into play. These are the occasional mental factors, including applied attention, sustained attention, decision, energy, curiosity, and motivation. When the mind is deliberately focused on a particular object instead of just letting it go on its own way, when we deliberately keep it trained on an object or even when we try to let the mind wander free, we are imposing some control on the process, and it is no longer completely subject to unconscious forces. The universal processes, such as attention and focus, become intentional.

> **The factors of decision, energy, curiosity, and motivation are what modulate the universal process of intention.**

The factors of decision, energy, curiosity, and motivation are what modulate the universal process of intention. Generally speaking, the occasional processes arise when operating on the universals. Thanks to these processes, we can perform mental training (*bhavana*) or meditation. As directing the mind needs quite a lot of effort, this type of mental training is a discipline that requires patience and perseverance.

The universal and occasional cognitive processes are functional and ethically neutral, but most of the time they are accompanied by healthy or unhealthy affective processes. Those that generate mental states that lead to liberation from suffering are considered healthy, while the unhealthy ones tend towards greater conditioning and less awareness.

The unhealthy processes are ignorance, uneasiness, impudence, audacity, attachment, aversion, identification, worry, pride, envy, avarice, dejection, laziness, and doubt. Usually, we are not aware that we are under their influence, in which case the universal factors appear together with the unhealthy factors without the participation of the occasional factors.

Other times occasional factors are present and we act detrimentally, even when we know we are doing so. When cognitive activity is dominated by the unhealthy processes, we really do not care if we are acting in a harmful way—we can even be trapped by the power and gratification that this unhealthy process induces. On other occasions we may be aware of the unhealthy states by applying sustained attention—we may be aware, for instance, of aversion—but this awareness will not be transformative and will only serve to perpetuate the aversion. Attention must be deliberate for the cognitive activity (*citta*) to be healthy. (See Figure 9.)

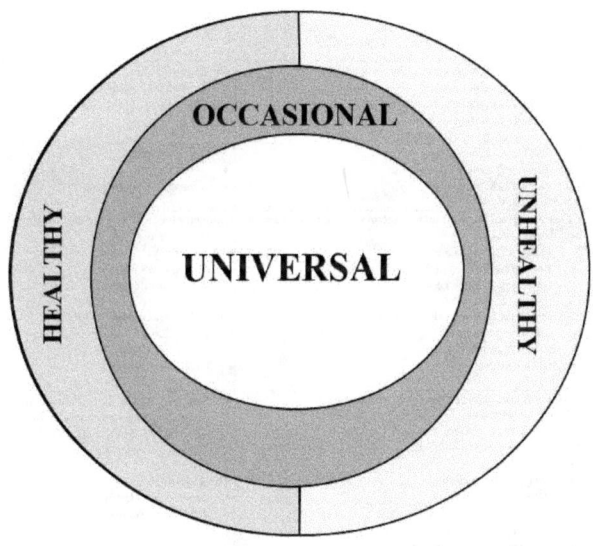

Figure 9: The structure of a moment of consciousness.

Healthy cognitive processes can be classified on a progressive scale. Some are considered universal—common to any healthy cognitive activity—and can include, for example, mindfulness, dignity, consideration for others, and trust. Other cognitive processes are considered roots, given that they are healthy responses to desire, and can include non-attachment, non-aversion, and composure. There are also healthy cognitive processes

Integral Vipassana

which affect both somatic and cognitive activity, such as serenity, clarity, flexibility, adaptability, efficiency, and integrity.

Among the healthy cognitive processes are the three ethical elements of the Buddha's method—harmonious speech, harmonious action, and harmonious life. There are also processes considered to be extraordinary qualities of the mind, such as compassion, gratitude, or shared joy.

Lastly, we have the process that embodies the true objective of the Buddha's method: wisdom.

Figure 10 shows the fifty-two mental factors mentioned in the Theravada tradition, organized into the categories that make up each moment of consciousness (*citta*): universal, occasional, healthy, and unhealthy.

Sabbacittasādhāraṇa **Universal**	• *Fassa* - Contacting, connecting • *Vedanā* - Feeling • *Saññā* - Recognizing, perceiving • *Cetana* - Intending	• *Ekaggata* - Mental focus • *Jīvitindriya* - Vitality • *Manasikāra* - Mental attention
Pakiṇṇaka **Occasional**	• *Vitakka* - Choosing • *Vicara* - Examinining • *Adhimokkha* - Deciding	• *Viriya* - Effort • *Pīti* - Rapture • *Chanda* - Commitment
Akusala **Unhealthy**	**Four universal harmful mental factors -** *Akusalasādhāraṇa* • *Moha* - Illusion • *Ahirika* - Lack of shame • *Anottappa* - Comtempt for consequences • *Uddhacca* - Restlessness **Three mental factors in the cupidity group -** *Lobha* • *Lobha* - Covetousness • *Diṭṭhi* - Incorrect belief • *Māna* - Arrogance	**Four mental factors in the hatred group -** *Dosa* • *Dosa* - Hate • *Issa* - Envy • *Macchariya* - Avarice • *Kukkucca* - Remorse **Other harmful mental factors** • *Thīna* - Sloth • *Middha* - Lethargy • *Vicikiccha* - Doubt
Sobhana **Healthy**	**Nineteen admirable universal mental factors -** *Sobhanasādhāraṇa* • *Saddhā* - Confidence • *Sati* - Constant mindfulness • *Hiri* - Dignity • *Ottappa* - Responsability • *Alobha* – Non-cupidity • *Adosa* – Non-hatred • *Tatramajjhattatā* - Balance, mental neutrality • *Kāyapassaddhi* - Somatic serenity • *Cittapassaddhi* - Mental peace • *Kāyalahutā* - Lightness of body • *Cittalahutā* - Lightness of mind • *Kāyamudutā* - Somatic pliancy • *Cittamudutā* - Mental pliancy • *Kāyakammaññatā* - Wieldness of body • *Cittakammaññatā* - Wieldness of consciousness	• *Kāyapāguññatā* - Somatic flexibility • *Cittapāguññatā* - Mental flexibility • *Kāyujukatā* - Somatic regulation • *Cittujukatā* - Mental regulation **Three abstinences -** *Virati* • *Sammāvācā* - Harmonious speech • *Sammākammanta* - Harmonious behabior • *Sammā-ājīva* - Harmonious way of life **Two boundless states -** *Appamaññā* • *Karuṇā* - Compassion • *Mudita* - Sympathetic joy **One faculty of wisdom -** *Paññindriya* • *Paññā* - Wisdom

Figure 10: Each moment of consciousness (citta) is "colored" by some mental factors (cetasikas).

Citta Process and Concepts

The activity of *citta* starts out at the sensory gates (including the door to the mind). After passing through a "passive" phase controlled by the structured conditioning in the being (phylogenetics), it comes to a phase of "recognition of sensory data" from which it relates to uncountable individual conditionings (ontogeny) that make up a "perception." These are what we have so far called "bottom-up" and "top-down" processes. The passive phase has its hedonic assessment, and the reactive phase adds a healthy or unhealthy affective element, thus generating more conditioning. This is how conventional reality is constructed, based on conditioning that crystalizes into concepts, ideas, and thoughts.

It is important to realize that every sensory contact enters the mental process through its respective door. The shape makes contact with the eye and enters the mental process through the door of visual awareness. When you think about something from the past or in the future, or when you concentrate on thoughts or emotions, the cognitive process is arising through the door of the mind. Mental processes, which do not depend on previous sensory contact as do somatic processes, are faster.

As discussed earlier in this book, there is a "subtle materiality" to any kind of sensory contact—for example, in the sound that humans produce. The human scream uses the vibration of the vocal cords with a primary intentionality shared by the whole species. This intentional materiality has become specialized, generating codes that in turn have been structured into parts of the brain that are used to process all sound information in linguistic form. Thus, sound vibration diversifies and turns into a mental representation. These representations lead to shared signs and symbols and, through repetition, become code. In this way, concepts can be objectified as symbols with meaning and become associated with other concepts. In a slow rollout phonetics, grammar, syntax, or semantics take shape as we share the knowledge of speech and language.

Language is constructed, among other reasons, to discriminate objects in space. The representation of space, for instance, is built up from the sensations of length, width, and height that we extract from the shape of the material.

Matter and Space

Both exterior objects and the air that surround us are matter—a combination of the four elements. However, when we observe objects, we do not view what is between them as matter, but rather as *space*. We build differences in matter out of sensations in a way that depends on the conditioning of the senses that has evolved and is phylogenetic. So, we differentiate objects in space and construct measurements, which are conventional abstractions used to develop mathematics. Calculation then becomes a way of interpreting the outside world, and then the inner world. Through this process, concepts develop a force of truth on which we base beliefs and develop our expectations. Nevertheless, words and concepts will never have a greater meaning than that of the experiences that generate them.

Thanks to the many aspects of perception, we can create the appearance of two-dimensional or even three-dimensional spaces on a plane—for example, drawing a square or cube on a piece of paper. Indeed, our perception of space allows us to move the body efficiently, recognizing distances and directions. As we have seen, one of the most important types of sensation is proprioception, or the ability to experience at any given moment the position of the body in space, volume, and movement.

When we practice Vipassana, proprioception occupies a privileged place in experience because it is an activity that occurs in the present moment with a minimum degree of conceptual elaboration. We contemplate immediate somatic experience, freeing it from unnecessary considerations that get in the way of direct experience.

In the same way, when we contemplate sound, we are not interested in meaning or other linguistic characteristics, but rather the simple concatenation of the audible sensory impressions that are taking place at that moment.

This brings us to another key concept, time. This concept arises from the verification of the understanding of the *namarupa* process. First one thing, and then the other. There is a material aspect to time that can be seen in the alternation of light and dark (day and night), or in changes to the body (childhood, maturity, old age). There is also a temporal order to our activities, such as eating, working, sleeping, meditating, resting, etc. We are aware of chronological time, biological time, functional time, and the temporal process. Out of these arise the concepts of the past, present, or future, and with them memories, plans, and expectations.

Conditioned Cognitive Activity

For the Buddha, the activity of knowing is conditioned by the belief that the senses detect objects that then pass to the mind—in other words, that in the exterior world there is some kind of preexisting concrete reality to which we can relate. This belief in an external world that we capture through the senses may incline us to perceive any other view as incorrect—or at least to consider any such view as limited and imperfect.

According to this viewpoint, reality is outside and there is only one correct way of capturing it. The conventional perception attributes a unique concrete reality to what arises in the mind based on sensory stimuli. This process is automatic and unconscious, and the conclusions are entirely convincing. They are clearly and effortlessly presented with no room for any doubt. In reality, both the sensation and the feeling—that is to say *the contact and its affective interpretation*—are conditioned. They do not capture a reality that is out there but rather construct it from their own conditioning.

There is also cognitive conditioning in abstract mental objects. Take, for instance, a drawing of a cube with its eight vertices and twelve edges. There is not a moment's doubt, when seeing or imagining an object like this, in understanding it as a cube. This is how we automatically attribute an immediate and concrete reality to abstract objects. Remarkably, as we observe the image, we can clearly see different cubes. We only need to change the focus for cubes to appear that are different from the concrete reality of the drawing. There is no change in the object, just a change in the viewpoint. So another form of cognitive conditioning is to attribute an immediate, automatic, and concrete reality to abstract objects.

Conventionally, an object is considered to exist only because of its characteristics. The notion of object presupposes a separation between subject and object, as well as the conviction that there are properties that belong only to one and not to the other. According to this conditioning, things exist because of their characteristics—that is to say, the object has a number of attributes that the subject captures.

Let us imagine that when we hit a table with our hands, what we hear is the sound of the table. Similarly, if we hit a wall, we hear the sound of the wall, and if we hit our body, we hear the sound of our body. However, when we clap, we do not say that what we hear is the sound of a single hand. Up until that final action, our interpretation was that the sound belonged to the object we hit, that it was a characteristic of the object. Our hand was the subject that hit an object. However, in this final case, subject and object are inseparable.

This is the subtlest form of conditioning of the cognitive process—implicitly attributing a separate reality to objects and to the observer. All the characteristics to be found in objects can be nominated, classified, etc., and are the result of this type of simplification. The observer recognizes that the object has its own characteristics but cannot see that any characteristic is only an automatic interpretation of a phenomenon that occurred in a process of the *namarupa* relationship. There is no such thing as separate subject and object, but rather a succession of activities that give rise to an experience.

This form of mental conditioning is continuously occurring in all "rational" and "verbal" activity. What is more, language is structured in a way that reinforces the separation between the object and the subject observing it.

Ultimately, cognitive activity is conditioned activity, whether it be sensory or abstract experience. Conditioning includes the naive use of reasoning and language, which are all interpreted in an absolutist sense, as if they were the only truth.

The change in perspective that the Buddha proposes is to consider the activities of knowing as being generators of experience. There is no concrete external reality—only the relationship between different types of physical and mental data. The relationship or integration of this data is what builds an experience. Nonetheless, this relationship is also conditioned.

> **There is no concrete external reality—only the relationship between different types of physical and mental data.**

Tactile experience, for example, is a conditioned experience. Let us take some clay and shape it into a cup. There is an instant when the piece of clay *becomes* a cup. The matter is the same in both cases, and the tactile experience as well, but the unformed clay has disappeared and a cup has appeared in its place. The only thing that has changed is the mental activity, which now calls the clay a cup and attributes other characteristics to it.

For Buddha's *Dhamma* there are relative truths that are contextual. In other words, they may be unambiguous, useful, correct, and experimentally verifiable, but they also have limited validity. The relative truths about a cup include the following: it can be used for drinking or for holding flowers; if it falls to the ground, it breaks; it is made of clay. However, for the *Dhamma*, the absolute truth about a cup is that it does not exist by itself, independently, but that it is a concept or cognitive construct (*paññatti*).

Another conditioned way of associating phenomena is indirect contact—that is to say, setting limits to or delimiting an object (for example, by light). Given that there is light, the activities of knowing can "see" the shape of the object. But when we observe things around us or we look at our body, we do not take into account the conditions that allow the activity of delimiting. What we "see" is not the separate object but rather the interaction between the object, the light radiation, and the sense of sight, although this interaction is hidden. In this type of conditioned relationship, many conditions are invisible—both in the construction of the object and in conventional language.

The cognitive context of the object is obscured, and the mind limits itself to classifying. The mind projects the unconscious image that we hold of each object, an image that has arisen according to the circumstances. Most of the mental activity is dedicated to classifying, in other words pigeonholing the object in one of the previously existing definition categories. The very creation of the cognitive context of an object is a very occasional activity that we usually call "creative activity."

Teachers do not see people, they see students; salespeople see customers; mothers see children. Everyone is right. They all are operating correctly inside their roles. However, by operating like this, all are unable to see options outside of their "referential frameworks" or cognitive contexts, which were previously applied unconsciously and often created through study or training. Because human beings communicate on the basis of quite complex and subtle referential frameworks, instruction or teaching is needed for abstract and symbolic communication to be carried out in a manner more fitting to the convention.

Since referential frameworks are convenient and work very well in a conventional world, it makes no sense to search out other alternatives. We can say that another way to generate compound phenomena is to "construct" them through the unconscious choice of the referential framework.

Yet another conditioned form of relating to an object is "denomination"—to name it, and refer to it by words. When we do this, we are implicitly assuming its separate existence. We are creating "separate objects." The very syntax of the Indo-Aryan languages, with their verbs, subjects, predicates, etc., requires that we talk about "isolated" objects, and so the verbal form itself establishes a referential framework that cannot be overridden inside itself.

Sati is Cognitive Activity

Mindfulness (*sati*) is one of the healthy cognitive processes. In the manner that the different cognitive processes appear, we can track the development of *sati*, or constant conscious attention. Basic attention (included in universals) is trained by deliberate, conscious attention to occasional processes (applied and sustained), until it becomes complete attention (*sati/mindfulness*), which is considered a universal and healthy mental process. So, *sati* is the requisite for the rest of the healthy cognitive processes to develop. For the cognitive activity (*citta*) to be healthy, *sati* must be present.

Healthy cognitive activity always occurs accompanied by the universal healthy cognitive processes. When *sati* is present without moments of negligence, it will be accompanied by a complete belief that the experience can become free of suffering, as well as by dignity, self-respect, and consideration or respect for all beings that live through feeling activities. All mental patterns can be experienced thanks to *sati*, which heeds the rising or ceasing of any of them.

When there is *sati*, the emotional tone, the intentional posture, and the attitude with which one contemplates the object are rooted in non-greed, non-aversion, and non-confusion. This functionally excludes from the mind the opposites, the three poisons (avarice, aversion, confusion).

With these qualities, somatic and cognitive activities take on some special qualities—tranquility, clarity, flexibility, adaptability, efficiency, and honesty. If healthy attention can be sustained moment by moment, then the entire flow of consciousness is purified of its toxins and the rest of the healthy processes are reinforced, while their unhealthy counterparts wither. Full attention to unhealthy states is transformative precisely because the unhealthy quality of attention has been replaced by healthy attention, which influences both body and mind.

> **If healthy attention can be sustained moment by moment, then the entire flow of consciousness is purified of its toxins.**

The transformation that starts out with constant, confident, dignified, and respectful attention roots out avidity, aversion, and confusion from cognitive activity, generating a body/mind that is calm, clear, flexible, adaptable, efficient, and honest. With this foundation, harmonious speech, action, and lifestyle emerge effortlessly, producing joy for the well-being of others and compassion for their discomfort. Wisdom has finally been attained.

Composite Phenomena and Ultimate Realities

When somatic experience is observed, this reveals its ultimate components (solidity, temperature, cohesion, and pressure). In much the same way, cognitive experience can also be observed down to its fundamental categories of cognition (*citta*) and its processes (*cetasikas*). In the third foundation of attention, we are interested in discriminating between apparent, conventional, or compound reality (*paññati*), and the ultimate or irreducible reality (*paramattha*).

> **The factors of decision, energy, curiosity, and motivation are what modulate the universal process of intention.**

Ideas, concepts, or language are *paññatti*, while materiality (*rupa*), knowing (*citta*), and the cognitive processes (*cetasikas*), as well as *Nibbana*, are considered "ultimate realities" (*paramattha dhamma*). The material elements (*rupa*), cognition (*citta*), perception, nonattachment, or avarice (*cetasikas*) are realities that maintain their characteristics (non-attachment is not and cannot be avarice, temperature is not and cannot be solidity), which is why they are considered ultimate realities.

These ultimate realities (*paramatthas*) result from the correctly realized analysis of experience. On the other hand, our conventional reality includes everything that seems real to us, including living beings, people, men, women, animals, and the seemingly stable objects that constitute our immediate experience of the world, but are in fact constantly changing characteristics.

Concepts are apparent realities (*paññatti*), and therefore are impermanent and unsatisfactory. Strictly speaking, *paramatthas* are also conditioned realities (*sankhara*) as only *Nibbana* is unconditioned, but they are not compound like *paññatti*.

The practice of Vipassana leads to the understanding that all *sankharas* are impermanent and unsatisfactory, including *rupa*, *citta*, and *cetasikas*, and that all *dhammas* or phenomena of experience do not belong to the experiencer, as they are activities that arise from the evolutionary process. To put it another way, they are not "I."

Contemplating the Concept of "I"

As discussed in this book's Preface, a central concept in Vipassana is contemplation of the "I." When cognition is centered on the idea of "I," it cannot go beyond logical thinking. In the *Dhamma*, this belief in the "I" is considered an "erroneous perspective," and ridding ourselves of this belief is the "correct perspective," which leads to wisdom.

Contemplation with *sati* reveals that thoughts, sensations, feelings—sometimes of pain and sometimes of pleasure—follow one another. Practice leads to the subsidence of conceptualization and to the direct experience of these phenomena as transitory processes. Experience neither needs the interference nor the centrality of the "I." When "I" tries to explain it to itself, it realizes that reasoning returns it to conceptualization, and this causes doubts. Only experience clears doubts. Wisdom leads to greater calm and in turn to greater wisdom.

> **Although the concept of "I" can be useful for linguistic communication, when we turn it into something real, permanent, and absolute, it causes much suffering.**

Sometimes we tend to visualize things during meditation, such as deities or "buddhas." We create them with the mind and end up believing they are real. When visualizations are recognized as concepts and appear in meditation, they do not become the goal of meditation, but rather reveal the underlying processes.

Although the concept of "I" can be useful for linguistic communication, when we turn it into something real, permanent, and absolute, it causes much suffering.

We have also seen that the conventional view (or relative truth according to *Dhamma*) starts from assumptions that affirm the following:

the subject-object distinction, an "I"/other limit that generates individual identity, as well as the centrality and sovereignty of individuality.

This belief in the "I" includes specific psychological limits, an illusion of control, and a desire to manipulate the outside world for its own personal purposes. When the self is understood correctly as being a cognitive construct, a representation, many of the supposedly essential "problems" of life lose their importance.

The "I" is, in fact, a fiction, an abstraction of the mind that we continue to build throughout our lives. The follower of the path of *sati* is able to observe and understand mental processes without the need for an "I" at the center of experience. There is thought, there is feeling, and there is perception emerging and ceasing, but these activities do not need a substantial "I" as controller, except as a linguistic convention.

> **The "I" is a fiction, an abstraction of the mind that we continue to build throughout our lives.**

As a matter of fact, there is nothing authentic in "I"—it is merely a belief. This understanding is at the heart of the truth of Buddha's *anatta*, or "non-self."

The problem is that just as soon as we attach labels and concepts to something, the self begins to objectify them, to establish them conclusively, to create fantasies and turn them into something static and permanent. And this is where the illusion starts. We believe the "I" to be real, as this is the reference that culture and society give to the level of complexity of the system, which means that we have to construct concepts using high-level abstractions.

The sensation stage kick-starts the construction of the notions of "I" (subject) and "mine" (object), and this duality is maintained until it crystallizes completely and stays at the conceptual level. However, we do not recognize it as abnormal because the subject-object relationship is the basis of cognition. So, what starts out as a complex physiological process that has emerged conditionally soon develops into a conceptualization between the subject and the object—a duality.

The "I" concept is the source of the complex cognitive process and serves as a convenient symbolic mechanism. In fact, self-concept is a cognitive construct. Cognition involves all the processes through which sensory information is transformed, reduced, elaborated, stored, recovered, and used. In other words, every psychological phenomenon is a cognitive phenomenon and refers to the activities of knowing.

Achieving a transcendent state of calm, devoid of an illusion of "owning oneself," is the aim of psychological training, or *bhavana* (mental cultivation). What the Buddha discovered upon awakening was that, in opposition to a static and inherent "I," there is only a changeable flux that becomes "I," constantly fed by perceptions, and this does not represent a static entity to which everything belongs.

Nevertheless, mental and material processes arise so that it seems to the "I" that experiences are continuous and permanent. In addition, these processes are made up of so many characteristics or phenomena interwoven by complex conditioning that they appear to be a whole piece. The different types of consciousness (visual, auditory, etc.), each of which has its specific functions and importance, appear as a unit, thereby creating a complete scenario. The process is so quick, and the different objects appear and disappear at such speed, that it has all the appearance of a film, but real. This very speed turns small, unhealthy reactions into misperceptions and hallucinations.

To sum up, the activity of knowing is to receive a conditioned stimulus and interpret it, thus conditioning the next contact. The process happens so fast that it gives the illusion of continuity.

The Basis of the Mind and the Portal to the Mind

Our heart contains an autonomous, well-developed nervous system of over 40,000 neurons, plus a complex and dense network of neurotransmitters, proteins, and support cells. Thanks to such elaborate circuits, it would seem that the heart can initiate cognitive processes and can also learn, remember, and even perceive. Four types of connections that start in the heart and that reach the central nervous system have so far been observed: neurological, biochemical, biophysical, and energetic.

By transmitting nerve impulses, the heart sends more information to the brain than it receives. It is the only bodily organ with this property, and it can inhibit or activate certain parts of the brain, depending on circumstances. The heart can also influence our perception of reality and, therefore, our reactions. It ensures the overall balance of the body—*homeostasis*—through hormones and neurotransmitters. One of its effects is to inhibit the production of the stress hormone but also to produce and release oxytocin, known as the love hormone. The heart interacts with the rest of the body through its rhythm, its variations, and what are known as pressure waves. The heart is the first organ to process information, which is then passed onto other systems. Additionally, the heart's electromagnetic field is the strongest of all the organs in the body—some sixty times more intense than that of the brain—and it has been observed to change depending on emotional state. When we feel afraid, frustrated, or stressed, it is chaotic.

Conventionally there are two kinds of heart-rate variations. One is harmonious with expansive regular waves and occurs when a person has positive and generous emotions and thoughts. The other is very irregular with incoherent waves and appears alongside negative emotions such as fear, ire, or distrust. Brain waves become synchronized to these variations in heart rate—in other words, *the heart does rule the mind!*

It's almost like the heart has a brain of its own, which activates the true brain's higher centers of perception. These in turn are able to interpret reality without having to resort to past experiences. When the heart's activity is integrated into the rest of the body, it creates a state of biological coherence—everything is harmonious and works correctly. This integration is propitiated through positive emotions—openness to others, listening, patience, cooperation, acceptance of differences in others, freedom from fear. All are deeply rooted in human beings, as they have served us well to survive many thousands of years.

It is convenient to differentiate between the base and the door of each sense. Although there is a door for each sense, any cognitive activity causes consciousness to cease by default, or *bhavanga*. This is the consciousness that always appears whenever cognitive activity is stopped. It appears between cognitive processes, when there is no intentional activity, during sleep without dreams, or in a coma. Therefore, cognition and *bhavanga* are mutually exclusive—activity by one stops the activity of the other. Nevertheless, *bhavanga* is a type of awareness that is able to maintain basic survival activities. It does not seem, therefore, that it is an empty consciousness, but rather a basal consciousness characteristic of each organism. In this sense, it would appear to be the manifestation of consciousness in a specific organism, its function to maintain vital continuity. *Bhavanga* may be the most stable activity of a living being.

Citta includes all that has access to consciousness—somatic, affective, subjective or phenomenological awareness, mental, or cognitive.

Self-Transcendence

Here lies the possibility of transcendence for humans. We humans can rise above our own productions in a process of abstraction that includes the elements from one level but transcends them. When we understand how physical processes work, we can learn to choose the best behavior for survival and reproduction. Understanding the affective conditioning that we are subject to, we can change the rigid response that obliges us to retain the pleasant and avoid the unpleasant. When we realize that all actions, physical or mental, have consequences, we can then anticipate and generate mental representations in order to design strategies and choose objectives.

Buddha's great discovery was to understand that the mind can transcend its own activity, and that wisdom resides in developing these possibilities of self-transcendence. Self-transcendence is the understanding of the non-substantiality of "I"—that is to say, the understanding that "I" is a concept or mental construct, and not a substance with its own existence. The activity of knowing, whether it be *citta* or *bhavanga*, is the only thing that has continuity, while bodies and their activities of feeling, conceptualizing, or realizing are merely transitory.

Citta is data processing, physical or mental. A mental sensation has the same process as one that is physical; the difference is that the former does not require contact with the physical object. Logically, mental processing is faster than sense processing. However, we may perceive and evaluate a mental sensation, giving it an intentional dimension. In short, mental sensations are also conditioned. As mental data are evaluated and cause reactions, a conditional relationship is established between them.

Each *citta* (process of knowing) not only includes an affective assessment but is also always accompanied by mental activities which confer upon it different qualities. There are activities that always accompany *citta* and others that appear due to circumstance or conditioning.

Sati (mindfulness) may be present in the flow of *cittas*, and with its presence reveals the construction or reification that the mind carries out of the knowing processes. Human beings can be aware of their perceptions, their intentions, their feelings, their sensations, their degree of energy and mental acuity, and even their level of attentiveness.

By becoming aware of its activities, the mind can turn them into its tools. It can focus and sustain attention on a voluntarily chosen object or activity. It can have motivations or conscious intentions, show determination when pursuing goals, and make an effort to work well and become highly enthusiastic. This possibility of paying attention to its own activities leads to the illusion that the "I" is what builds and controls them. Learning from past experiences implies having memory and intention—in other words, selecting answers based on an objective.

Sati, by penetrating the learning mechanisms, reveals that the choice of responses produces conditioning, and this entails memory of past reactions.

We must remember that the root of the word *sati* is memory. This is probably one of the most hotly debated topics of the Buddha's model. Scientific psychology considers basic psychological processes in the same way that *Dhamma* considers universal mental factors (*cetasikas*) that accompany any knowing activity. However, memory does not appear among these. The only reference to memory is *sati*.

Mindfulness and the Memory of Oneself

One of the most controversial questions amongst those who study the *Dhamma* is the omission of memory in the Buddha's psychological model.

One must be careful when drawing parallels between two psychological models that start from different premises and that have different objectives, as is the case with the *Dhamma* and scientific psychology. Nevertheless, *sati*, with its etymological root of "memory," is the only reference in the Buddha's teachings to the basic psychological process that experimental psychology calls memory.

In psychology, *attention, perception,* and *memory* are considered to be basic psychological processes, and even though they try to differentiate between these functions in the construction of lived experience, they are processes which overlap. The basic processes include *emotion* and *motivation*, which represent the affective part; *learning*, which is the process in charge of associating stimuli with behaviors; and *behaviors* with their consequences.

Additionally, *thought* and *language* are viewed as complex processes in comparison with those mentioned above, which are classified as simple. These eight processes are, in turn, concepts that hold specific meanings in our psychological culture and that will be active in our understanding of the Buddha's psychological model.

In recent decades, theories and research from the field of cognitive neuroscience on how memory functions have undergone important changes. Faced with the natural tendency to simplify the concept as if it were a single system, these days we speak instead of different types of memory that have different logics, different functions in cognitive activity, and are located in different areas of the brain.

A useful way to explain this complexity is to begin by separating "short-term memory" from "long-term memory." Even though both are involved in building the ongoing experience, their role is different.

Sati, as memory, seems to refer to "remembering the present moment." Among the three psychological qualities that must be developed on the Buddha's Noble Eightfold Path, *sati* includes and transcends *samadhi*—that is to say, it is free from attraction and repulsion—and *samadhi* likewise includes and transcends *vayama*. In other words, *sati* is able to manage the level of activation of the organism (body/mind). It is "moment-to-moment attention" freed from attraction and repulsion, as well as from agitation or lethargy. *Sati* is aware of the focus and level of attention activation at all times. This relationship with time is what makes *sati* a perfect candidate to occupy the function of memory (and, specifically, short-term memory) in the Dhamma.

Within short-term memory you can make a distinction between *sensory memory* and *working memory*. Sensory memory is what the senses perceive and lasts between 0.2 and 0.3 seconds. It appears that we cannot be aware of a sensory stimulus lasting less than 0.5 seconds, which would imply that an enormous number of sensory contacts do not even become potentially conscious. This means there is a drastic limitation on the information that the organism uses when dealing with reality; it also means that what we call "the present" is subject to a specific chronological time scale.

The information that becomes potentially conscious in sensory memory, however, is again limited when accessing working memory. This would appear to act as a buffer, holding a limited amount of data. The choice of data mainly depends on the attention systems, which prioritize some data over other. Today we know that working memory is not limited to merely receiving data but, as its very name suggests, is in fact capable of working with it.

Working memory has a limited capacity, as it can hold only a few items of information. This ability varies from person to person and is predictive of measurements of intelligence, reading skill, comprehension, or language acquisition. It is used in complex mental operations such as selecting, integrating, and updating information. In addition, it is rapidly exhausted when subjected to tasks that demand a high degree of attention, and it also degrades under conditions of stress or negative emotionality, as well as over time.

The Dimension of "Now"

There is no such thing as a present moment or a subjective experience of the present, but rather *momentary configurations* that are a product of the integration of multiple qualitatively sensory representations that are significantly different from what is occurring. Each sensory representation needs different and variable integration timescales. These integrate into a general representation that does not have a limited fixed length of time and may last several seconds.

> There is no such thing as a present moment or a subjective experience of the present.

It is the dimension of "now," consisting of superimposing momentary configurations of sensory integration, that gives us the sensation of continuity. The experience of "now" can last several seconds and includes alternatives, reasons, and the anticipation of consequences, determined by "who I am" or "who I believe I am"—my knowledge, my aims, my values, or my beliefs. Some neurocognitive researchers have called this succession of "nows" a *continuity field* since these discrete packages of experience may seem continuous.

The specific content of this integration pack is updated as and when sensory processes produce new information. These processes function more by information capacity limits than by time limits. In other words, the package contents are not synchronously updated, but rather there are partial updates that produce a coherent version of what is happening. The previous package interferes with the following one to give the sensation of coherence and continuity, even if this means it does not accurately reflect the external object. It would seem that the system is set up to give us a sense of stability, although to this end it manipulates the incoming information and makes predictions based on experience accumulated in long-term memory.

In brief, the working memory is where "now" is constructed and produces the sense of continuity and sovereignty of "I" that leads us to experience it as being "reality" or "my reality." Working memory is where attention and memory mediate to generate perception. These are the simple basic psychological processes previously mentioned.

Perception, despite being the product of processing, is just part of what we call experience. Furthermore, as we will see later, thought and language, as well as emotion and motivation, all play a role in perception. Learning happens when we convert the fluid cognition that is characteristic of short-term memory into crystallized cognition in long-term memory.

The "Present" in Dhamma

In the *Dhamma* there are also these different versions of the 'present' (*paccuppanna*). Momentary present (*khana paccuppanna*) only covers the three phases of a moment of consciousness (*citta*)—arising, being, and ceasing. We relate it with "sensory memory," and in this sense, it is the closest to the 'present,' even if it does not become conscious.

In fact, in the *Dhamma*, the cognitive process that allows a piece of sensory data to be recorded requires a series of up to seventeen *cittas* that follow a predetermined order. This cognitive mini-process is called *vithi*. Even so, this is an isolated sensory data that has to become cognitive in order to be operational. In the *Dhamma* this conversion from sensory to mental is called "grasping the past." Nevertheless, this cognitive data is still not enough to generate experience.

> **In Dhamma there is no fixed point—experience is constructed of activities inside activities and cycles that overlap each other.**

The cognitive data related to a "sensible object" (a horse, for example) are organized into a series of cognitive processes (*vithis*) relative to the object, until a "thing concept" (*atthapaññatti*) arises, the experience of something that is still unnamed. Giving it a name is the last step of the process—when one thinks 'a horse' it becomes a name-concept (*nama-paññatti*). Each *citta* arises due to the contact (*phassa*) between something sensible and the receiving sense, but the sensory data that become mental may be used later without the need for sensory contact. In the *Dhamma* human beings possess six senses, so these data "abstracted" from the five senses are the "objects" of the sixth sense.

All these processes, which take just milliseconds, are integrated into a general representation, the "now," which in the *Dhamma* is called "present in series" (*santati paccuppanna*). However, it must be remembered that these activities are not written on a blank sheet, but rather inside the framework of a flow of functional activities (*kiriya*), conditioned by previous intentional activities (*kamma-vipaka*). What makes the psychological model of the *Dhamma* difficult to understand is that there is no fixed point—experience is constructed of activities inside activities and cycles that overlap each other.

Yet we must not forget that the *Dhamma* is an ethical psychology where psychological well-being depends on the affective and moral quality of our actions, words, and thoughts. As a matter of fact, *citta* is translated both as *heart* and as *mind*, keeping the term *manas* to refer to the intellect. Each *citta* involves the so-called "universal mental factors" but also other affective factors which may be healthy or not.

Whether this contact leads to sensory awareness or not (0.5 sec.) depends on the attention given—in other words on the duration (*manasikara*), focus (*ekkagata*), and vitality (*jivitindriya*), which are—precursors of *sati*, *samadhi*, and *pañña*. The presence of *citta* is associated with a hedonic assessment (*vedana*), which gives it a tendency or an intention (*cetana*) and entails a mark of perception (*sañña*) that contributes to the experience (*viññana*). As we have remarked before, as each *citta* arises, it is accompanied by healthy or unhealthy factors and by other occasional ones.

As in the case of working memory in cognitive psychology, the resulting experience depends on the previous moment and on "who I believe I am." It uses both "attended to" and "recovered" information. The *Dhamma* adds an affective-ethical factor in the shape of healthy or unhealthy factors, which appear depending on their *hedonic* (bodily pleasure and pain) or *eudaimonic* value (good and bad—that is to say, values and virtues that are always in juxtaposition to their opposites, moral poverty and vices). Thus, not only do actions and speech have consequences on current bodily well-being, but so do thoughts and cognitive activities in general. This means that it is possible to learn how to keep the organism (body/mind) in good shape.

Working Memory and the Continuity Field

Working memory functions in this *continuity field* (as defined in cognitive neuroscience) or "present in series" (*Dhamma*), which is the result of integrating an immense amount of information. Continuity is the way of making a pandemonium of processes, all taking place at different speeds, temporally coherent. The conscious experience, what we live as reality, is built on working memory and depends on attentional activity (*sati, samadhi, vayama*).

If we focus attention on the result of the process—that is to say, on the content of the experience, as if it were "reality"—our ability to act is limited to interpreting it by offering an opinion on that reality.

If, on the other hand, we focus on the interior of the "continuity field," then we reach an intimate experience—the "how am I experiencing reality," or the physiological, affective, and conceptual aspects of which it is made. (Now there is tension, agitation, relaxation, calm, anger, sadness, kindness, joy, etc.)

If we reach "how I am constructing reality"—the process of building subjectivity—then we must admit that this reality is only one of many possible perspectives, which is when decentering occurs. We then comprehend that what appears as reality is no more than one possible configuration of a particular and situated reality. In other words, it is not "I," but a transitory experience resulting from a specific physiological state, affective preferences, and underlying intentions. Thus, transcendence of "my point of view" occurs.

While the first scenario is an "ego-centered" position that does not require access to working memory, the other two need the attentional processes to monitor those seconds where what we are going to experience as "reality" is being constructed. This highlights the importance of tuning into the levels of vigilance, focus, and continuity of attention. In the first scenario, which is the domain of *Samatha* meditation, we only need to pay attention to the content of the experience. The second is the domain of Vipassana meditation, and it involves transforming the way of producing the experience and changing the conditions and the causal relationships (understanding of conditionality) that create or sustain it, although this is accomplished without fixing, forcing, or doing something with great effort or "will."

> **Sati is to remember, without a moment's slip, what is happening in the working memory.**

Sati is to remember, without a moment's slip, what is happening in the working memory, and to that end it requires a stable focus on the continuity field. This stable focus (*samadhi*) is achieved thanks to an adequate level of vigilance, a harmonious, attentive energy or effort (*vayama*). When *sati* is continuous, which means that there is enough *samadhi* and *vayama*, then *piti* appears (enthusiasm, joy in the experience) along with *sukha* (satisfaction, an experience of plenitude).

However, current models of how the working memory functions suggest that verbal-phonological and visuospatial processes are processed separately, which may generate two competing "realities." So, when attention is focused on that period when the emergence of the experience is observed, it is a question of seeking a new balance between both realities, one conceptual and the other situational (an understanding of *nama* and *rupa*, mentality and materiality).

If the conceptual, linguistic, and literal reality is preferred, then identification with the "narrative self" happens, while if the visuospatial reality that includes sensory and kinesthetic aspects is preferred, then identification with the "experiential self" occurs. If the disidentification of the two selves does not occur, it may be believed that feeling is better than thinking, or that thinking is better than feeling.

> **When one realizes that any experienceable reality is only partial and accepts the inevitable partiality of experience, serenity ensues.**

Notwithstanding this, both perspectives are necessary and at work in Vipassana meditation. The narrative self needs to be embodied, and the experiential self needs to be discerning. The experiential self deals with spatio-temporal aspects and the narrative self with symbolic representations. The former deals with the concrete (the present conditions), and the latter with the abstract, which allows us to generalize, predict, and search for alternatives.

When one "takes charge of the feelings" that are happening "now," that person will avoid comparing "me" with "others." When the approach is "I take charge of the thoughts" that arise "now," that person realizes how and when they are using concepts to defend "me" from "others."

Furthermore, this framework of "believing that experience is truth" or "considering experience to be an interpretation of the truth" allows us to distinguish the level of psychological maturation. In the first case, "my reality" cannot be renounced because it is the only reality we can "see," while in the second we can understand the relativity of "my reality," which generates compassion towards ourselves and others. When one realizes that any experienceable reality is only partial and accepts the inevitable partiality of experience, serenity ensues.

Whichever the case, the process of building the experience continues regardless of the attention level. What we experience as reality arises out of inertia, even when attention is not focused on anything. This inertia asserts itself even on our intention or will to be attentive moment by moment. It can be seen in the phenomenon that has been called "mind wandering." We all experience these "thought drifts" that happen reactively and unconsciously, caused by sense data (a smell) or a mental image, which set off a chain of automatic physical and mental phenomena that return us to the state we previously characterized as "believing that experience is the truth."

As a matter of fact, there is no such mind wandering, just conditioning. Phenomena appear or disappear depending on how strong the connections that associate them are. In wandering there is perception, intention, and all the other activities needed for the experience, only now these are occurring at the organism's "basal" level (the level that acts as referential base for said organism—what the Abhidhamma calls bhavanga.) In the field of neuroscience, this bhavanga state to which the organism returns when it is not directed towards an object is called a default neural network. In this state, for example, conscious intentionality has been replaced by a self-referential conditioned intentionality. In other words, the system turns to "who I think I am," and the way in which the system relates to the exterior world is used to relate to oneself.

The attention focusing network and the default neural network are mutually exclusive. When attention is intentionally focused, the default neural network is suspended. On the other hand, if it is working, the focusing network stops. Given that the orientation network is associated with the active search for an "object" (i.e., with attraction and repulsion, or "affects") we can safely assume that the default neural network reflects the basal affective state of the organism, something like the satisfaction level with oneself.

Wandering is characterized by content dissociated from the immediate surroundings—situational aspects or sense data of the environment, and characterized as well by fluctuations in "meta-consciousness." This can happen with or without knowledge of this wandering. Nevertheless, not everybody with a prodigious working memory mind-wanders less than those with a lesser working memory. In fact, people with better working memory are more able to inhibit or permit mind-wandering, depending on how demanding the task at hand is.

Therefore, we should not necessarily consider mind-wandering to be a failure of attention, but rather view it as a necessary phenomenon that one learns to manage. What does seem true is that the increase in sati unifies and balances all attentional activity, thereby undoing the self-referential function of the default neural network. It is no longer necessary to relate to an "I" that has been deconstructed. Sati invalidates the need for a "memory of self" and so frees the organism (body/mind) from the conditioning process that generates suffering (dukha).

Training in *sati* limits reactivity to information in the working memory by processing more information that is relevant to the task and by limiting non-relevant information. Thus, working memory capacity can be strengthened—which, as we have seen, is fundamental to high-level cognitive activities.

Sati and Memory

Sati reveals the working memory, monitoring the physiological, affective, perceptual, and conditioned activities that constitute experience (aggregates). These aggregates are the necessary basis for the balance between insight, vitality, joy, peace, integration, and serenity (awakening factors) that characterize spiritual wisdom. *Sati*, therefore, has a fundamental role in working memory.

Morever, *sati*'s healthy qualities allow for a precise and efficient working memory through which conditioning and conscious deconditioning occur. When there is *sati*, there is causality. When there is one thing, another arises. Likewise, when something does not arise, the other does not arise either. We can see that there are causes and conditions. The conditions can be managed, but the causes are outside us and are not under the control of our will.

Intention, which is linked to physiological adaptation, can be directed towards other objectives and turn into motivation, a background driving force. When the mind becomes aware of intention, perception, and the other activities used for knowing, it embeds them into a timeline. The experience of a lived past and an anticipated future can feed the idea of an "I" by making the experience autobiographical, thereby raising awareness of a "self" capable of symbolic representations.

Primary Emotions

Mental representations are able to produce the same affective reactions as the contacts that they represent. In other words, if I imagine meeting a loved one, I feel happy because it is an important contact for me, even if it is not a probable occurrence. These reactions are what we call *primary emotions*, and they are important features of the mind precisely because they oblige us to plan actions—they have power over behavior. Primary emotions are the mental expression of the disturbances in the mind caused by feelings that originate both in sensations and in mental representations.

Secondary Emotions

In the Theravada tradition, which is what we have taken as our model, there are six primary emotions: attachment, aversion, ignorance, non-attachment, non-aversion, and non-ignorance. However, human life is a social life, and so we suppose that the other person is also experiencing emotions. Today, this is called *theory of mind*, or the ability to attribute thoughts and intentions to others. A new perspective of reality that includes others begins here—a perspective of "you" not as another, but as "another like me." It is the ability to put yourself in other people's shoes. By admitting the other person's emotions into our own emotional state, we generate secondary emotions.

The secondary emotional system includes imitation, empathy, prejudice, stereotyping, altruism, and the social bond. The whole range of comparative feelings such as pride, vanity, and envy are framed by the perspective of "you." This is the basis of the social and cultural norms that characterize our species. Thus, we build "we," "you," and "they." The brain and the nervous system are structured as a response to the need for integrating these levels. As we have seen before, in the tradition of the Buddha, the secondary emotions are midway between the healthy and unhealthy mental factors.

The Three Poisons

The *Sutta* states that one must be present when, in the activity of knowing, there is attachment, hatred, or obfuscation. We understand that as referring to the three unhealthy roots, also called the three poisons. They are the mental factors that arose from reacting to the affective assessment of pleasant, unpleasant, or neutral. The difference is, not only are they in sensations but also in mental representations, including "I" and the others.

The identity arising from the awareness of knowing is shaped by the affective, pleasant-unpleasant-neutral matrix, and it in turn modifies the activities of knowing, intention, memory, perception, etc. The loop created between mental activities and the awareness of them generates the illusion that it is "I" that directs them. To some extent this is true—since the mind has access to these activities, it also has the possibility of placing them at the service of that identity. The illusion lies in believing this "I" actually directs the activities, rather than simply being able to access them.

This illusion in the Buddha's *Dhamma* is known as "wrong vision," and is the cause of a great deal of human suffering. This wrong vision is constructed—that is to say, it is not innate, although it arises due to the primary impulse to seek out the pleasant and reject the unpleasant. The separation that arises from attachment ("I am this," "this is mine") and rejection ("I am not this," "this is not mine")—in other words, the identifications that construct the "I"—has emerged out of the history of rewards and frustrations when seeking the pleasant and rejecting the unpleasant, thereby forming a being which now believes in its own existence.

The affective processes inform the mental processes, but they not only accompany thought—they also order and guide behavior. *They define how we tend to act.* As previously seen, they reflect inclinations that have been selected by evolution and genetically transmitted. It appears that during the gestation process we somehow reproduce the evolutionary process of the species, as well as the changes and phylogenetic adaptations that have occurred from the activities of feeling. The set of supposedly inherited traits is temperament, the basis for personality. From this, *epigenetics*—or the influence on gene expression of how we react to the environment and to vital events or important events in life—shape character. Both temperament and character arise from the conditioning that occurs due to the activities of feeling or affection, which are what decide the development of the knowing activities.

> **Identity—the belief that character or temperament is "I"—becomes the key element in constructing perception.**

Identity—the belief that character or temperament is "I"—becomes the key element in constructing perception. We perceive from the perspective of what we believe to be and this identity is based on our memories of the past and our intention for the future. In the *Dhamma*, there is memory in sensation, in feeling, and in cognition, as they are all conditioned activities. However, the activity where all these memories are realized is *perception*, the activity that directly conditions experience.

Memory and Perception

Today there is a certain consensus around distinguishing between *declarative memory* and *non-declarative memory*. Declarative memory, or explicit memory, stores memories that can be consciously evoked. The contents of declarative memory can be brought to mind through propositions or images. It is a memory of facts.

Furthermore, declarative memory is divided into *episodic* and *semantic* memory. The episodic is a memory of past events in the subject's life that are dated in time, and is related to autobiographical memory. Semantic memory, however, refers to knowledge about the world and language.

Non-declarative or *procedural* memory, on the other hand, is a memory of skills related to knowing how to do things.

These two types of memory represent the two ways of acquiring self-knowledge that we humans use. We can learn from first-person experience, which is immediate and intuitive, or from third-person experience—that is to say, taking the content of first-person experience as an object. For example, I can realize that I react violently to criticism and try to resolve this, or I can spontaneously change these reactions after suffering as a result of them, without mediating a formulation of the problem, a reflection on it, or a plan to modify it.

Until recently it was thought that non-declarative memory was only procedural—automated procedures that could not be expressed in words and that only affected the area of movement. It is now increasingly obvious that it also refers to affective patterns, for instance certain aspects of attachment styles.

As we already saw when looking at feelings, desire is inscribed in biology. Innate relational modalities and those learned in childhood remain into adulthood, controlling much of our daily lives. The fact that emotional functioning is conditioned by these preverbal patterns is exactly what stops us from being able to access them through symbolic interpretation. By not depending on representations, these primary emotional patterns have no relation with "I," although they have shaped its existence. They therefore function as incoming information, as bottom-up processes. The non-declarative memory appears, consequently, to be integrated into the sensations and into primary, instinctive, or preverbal feelings.

Notwithstanding, declarative memory is representational and can be conscious or not, depending on how much attention we pay it. Declarative memory may be episodic, recreating sensory and space-time details of a memory, or semantic, which is what we use to represent the world in an organized fashion. Its contents are organized conceptually in function of the value or meaning given, or a causal relationship. While *sati* is part of what we now call working memory, and procedural memory is recorded in sensations, these other types of memory are activities of integrating perception.

Episodic memory is autobiographical and consists of sensory elements of a particular situation, while semantic elements are organized on hierarchical relationships of inclusion, belonging, or causality. Semantic memory generates and manages information that has not been explicitly learned, and which is implicit in its contents. In other words, it can make deductions.

It is interesting to note that information does not access the semantic memory from the episodic but rather through non-declarative memory. One of the most important characteristics of semantic memory is its affective relevance—things are remembered or not, depending on the affective value they may hold.

> **Only by acting ethically do you advance in mental stability. A healthy mind is a mind that is not conditioned by past unhealthy actions.**

Semantic memory adopts the point of view of an observer, whereas the episodic adopts that of the protagonist. It is what the *Sutta* refers to when it says that we have to observe externally, internally, as well as externally *and* internally, to understand that both positions coexist and are two perspectives of things. However, both concepts—internal and external—are underpinned by the belief in "I."

Perception and Intention

Intention loses its initial orientation towards survival or reproduction and instead seeks out objects or situations that give pleasure to the "I." By separating itself from its primary objectives, intention gives rise to personal ethics and collective morality. In Buddha's *Dhamma*, ethics (*sila*) holds a very important position. Indeed, in cultivating *sati*, *sila* occupies a fundamental position in so far as its development is directly related to mental stability (*Samadhi*). Only by acting ethically do you advance in mental stability. A healthy mind is a mind that is not conditioned by past unhealthy actions.

It is important not to convert Buddha's *Dhamma* into a moral ideology. When good and bad are established from the outside—what is called a *locus of external control*—the ethical maturity of people is curtailed. The *locus of internal control*—the conscious understanding of what is right or wrong in each context—is the path to an inclusive and universal ethic. When moral precepts are neither embraced nor integrated by the individual, and an external keeper/punisher is created, morality becomes just another problem for individual survival, and is not part of caring for oneself or one's surroundings. That would be a natural instinct for species that take care of their young.

Of course, we must be responsible for our actions in society, but to achieve this we have to be aware that we are beings guided by instinctively selfish impulses determined biologically. We must experience for ourselves that, in the face of individual vulnerability, the ethics of caring are more satisfactory than the ethics of law. When the origin of dissatisfaction is blamed on oneself, on the other, or on society, there is a lack of respect for oneself or others that is characteristic of a society that is degenerating. When we understand that dissatisfaction is due to the attachment, aversion, and ignorance that we share with many other beings, goodness then becomes the natural way to live. Although norms and laws are necessary, we have to travel the path of conscious attention, honestly facing the ethical decisions it entails, which may mean not necessarily obeying the established norms, rules, and rituals.

Perception and intention are the conditions for learning. To learn is to choose the right action for a given situation. Perception is the activity through which we define a situation. Perception, the result of the knowing activities, can be conscious, subliminal, or unconscious, depending on the contact and the context but, in any case, it is the definition of the situation from which voluntary behavior occurs. There is action to build perception and action consequent on perception. Action needs energy. Energy is a factor necessary for any activity and, in the Buddha's *Dhamma*, it is called "vital faculty" and refers to the vitality characteristic of any living being.

> When we understand that dissatisfaction is due to the attachment, aversion, and ignorance that we share with many other beings, goodness then becomes the natural way to live.

We must remember that living beings are those that are born and die, who are subject to a life cycle. From this point of view, the Buddha's *Dhamma* does not teach any kind of transcendence of life, but rather that liberation has to be something immanent to life. The mind can transcend somatic experience, and it can even transcend all its activities—but it cannot transcend life.

The Characteristics of a Free Mind

The rest of the paragraph of the *Sutta* dedicated to the mind refers to this transcendence of mental activities. If in the first foundation a distinction has been made between matter and mind, and in the second between carnal feelings and mental feelings, then in this third foundation there is a distinction between mental feelings and immaterial feelings. Mental feelings are still subtly subject to matter. When we say, "this mind has attachment" or "this mind has hate," it means that a mind with attachment or hate has repercussions on the body.

However, there are ways that the mind no longer has any kind of feeling about the body, which does *not* mean that the body is not continuing to function properly. If there is a mind that has attachment, hatred, or ignorance, then there can be a mind that does not have them—a mind free of attachment, rejection, or mental ignorance towards physical or knowledge activities. This is a mind at peace with physical and mental activities.

This step means that the body stops regulating the *citta* (consciousness) of each moment. *Citta* can be freed from sensual binding. However, this step also means transcending the desire to exist as a physical existence, and that poses a serious challenge. It is what other traditions call "dark night," as you have to suffer states of fear, insecurity, disenchantment, and restlessness. If all these states are transcended, then *citta* is experienced as the *Sutta* articulates.

The terms used in the various translations to refer to the qualities of the mind are different, and it is hard to know which are the most appropriate. Nevertheless, the mind knows when it is restricted and when it is relaxed—in other words it is experienced as a space. It knows when that space is limited and when it is unlimited. It knows when it has room for improvement and when not. It knows when there is only mind and when not. And it knows when it freed itself and when not. A mind free from the material is lived as infinite space, unlimited consciousness—an awareness of emptiness and of unified consciousness, a disappearance of the duality between the knower and the known. It is all about the mind in its purest state that is experienced through the immaterial *cittas*.

> **Suspending the activities of knowing provides serenity, calm, and ecstasy.**

The mind, thanks to *sati*, has learned to contemplate itself. It recognizes itself when it is restricted by too much concentration and when it does not have sufficient tone because it is too dispersed.

It knows when it has a global perspective and when its perspective is limited.

It understands if there are still residues of attachment, aversion, or ignorance.

It has itself as the sole object and knows when it has been released from any form of dissatisfaction.

It is important to remember that the mind has reached this point accompanied by *sati*. In the way that *jhanas* or meditative absorptions are understood in other traditions, they lead to the momentary disappearance of the knower-known duality. However, on the path of conscious attention, *sati* is a knowing activity.

In Summary

To know does not mean that there is a knower, but rather that there is an activity and a result. Suspending the activities of knowing provides serenity, calm, and ecstasy. Experiences of self-transcendence can be induced by different means, such as the ingestion of psychedelic substances, or even as a result of some type of accident that causes brain damage and the deactivation of certain parts of the brain. In all cases there is a reduction in self-related cortical brain activity.

Knowing also is a means to developing wisdom, but only the constant conscious attention of *sati* can attain the origin of existential dissatisfaction. The immature understanding of impermanence acquired in the early stages of meditation may give rise to the disappearance of duality, as can happen in a state of absorption or trance. However, such an experience does not lead to understanding and accepting the truth about the origin of dissatisfaction—instead, it tends to become an end in itself. To experience non-duality is part of the *sati* path, but not its objective.

4

CONTEMPLATION OF THE PHENOMENA OF EXPERIENCE

> "Monks, I will teach you the All. Listen &
> pay close attention. I will speak."
> "As you say, lord," the monks responded.
> The Blessed One said, "What is the All? Simply the eye & forms,
> ear & sounds, nose & aromas, tongue & flavors, body &
> tactile sensations, intellect & ideas. This, monks, is called the All.
> Anyone who would say, 'Repudiating this All, I will describe
> another,' if questioned on what exactly might be the grounds for
> his statement, would be unable to explain, and furthermore, would be
> put to grief. Why? Because it lies beyond range."
>
> Sabba Sutta: The All

In the three previous foundations, meditation is object-directed and voluntary—that is, planned. The meditator matures their body image, cultivates healthy states, or short-circuits the proliferation of self-referential thoughts. The meditator recognizes that their perception is limited, that their memories are biased, and that there are distortions and dysfunctional schemes in their cognitive function. The meditator realizes, therefore, that each behavior, word, or intention that is carried out in the organism has consequences. They know, ultimately, that they have a margin of freedom that can be expanded by getting rid of the conditioning, patterns, and habits that support the idea of "I am like this."

However, the meditator also recognizes that these habits and patterns are inscribed in the spontaneous activity of the organism (mind/body) without any voluntary or planned intervention. Then that person is prepared to attend the unfolding of the phenomena without getting involved with them. This is the meditation part of Vipassana itself.

Vipassana is the development of intuitive knowledge, the path of "insight," the transformation product of the "complete vision."

On this basis, the meditator realizes when there is intervention of the self and when there is not, when sensual desire or ill will arise and when they disappear, when there is agitation or torpor. Thus, they recognize when there are balanced states and when there are not, when and how the imbalance begins and when the balance returns. Furthermore, they recognize phenomena for what they are: physical sensations, hedonic appraisals, perceptions, reactive patterns and habits, and the very activity of knowing. That is, they recognize the activity of the "five aggregates"—the five types of activity in which the idea of "I" can be hidden. (See Figure 11.)

Thanks to this recognition, the meditator discovers that conditioning starts from the activity of the senses—not even the simple reception of information that occurs in the contact between the senses and their objects is free of conditioning.

By understanding how all that activity occurs, the organism (mind/body) can freely choose the activities that produce the greatest degrees of freedom, the factors that lead to liberation.

The process ends with the deep understanding of the Four Noble Truths: the verification of the dissatisfaction inherent in the human condition; the understanding that its origin is attachment (individual preferences or expectations); the vision of a way out of dissatisfaction; and the method for an effective realization of said way out.

As has been seen throughout the text, both the development of the first three foundations, which we call individual maturation, and the

Contemplation of the Phenomena of Experience

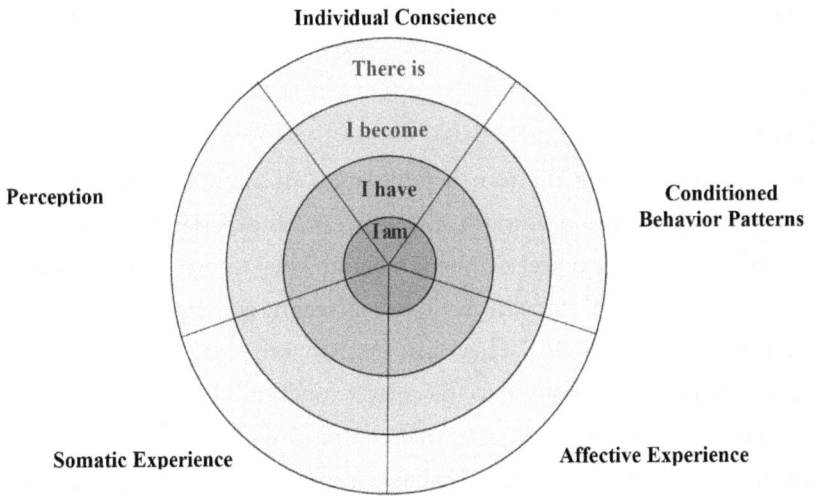

The Five Aggregates and the Twenty Wrong Views

	I am	I have	I become	There is
Sensing body				
Feeling				
Perception				
Mental formations				
Individual consciousness				

Figure 11: Work with the Five Aggregates consists of disidentifying the "I" from the twenty possible Wrong Views.

equanimous observation of the emergence and cessation of phenomena, which is characteristic of the fourth foundation and which we call *awakening*, work continuously. Paradoxically, individual maturation is the transcendence of the "I"—that is, the more maturity, the less "I." Spiritual awakening consists of suturing the separation between the "I" and the "other" and recognizing all possible states of consciousness until any form of subjectivity totally disappears. The process goes through states of absorption that are more ecstatic in some people and more serene in others. The disappearance of the belief in an "I" does not prevent social life, but provides a greater degree of freedom and, consequently, a decrease in suffering.

Experience

When contemplating the fourth foundation of attention, the meditator directs their attention towards the process of experience, rather than towards a particular object or phenomenon. They recognize when there is an excess or a lack of "knowing activity" or "feeling activity," or too much or too little "somatic activity." They also realize that the excess or lack of any of these activities is an obstacle to the correct functioning of *sati*.

The meditator realizes, too, that the process stagnates or accelerates depending on the level of attachment to sensations, feelings, perceptions, formations, or mental states.

Additionally, the meditator discovers that there are latent tendencies that condition the functioning of the very sensory bases, and that the body/mind organism cannot avoid these tendencies—indeed, it is dependent on external circumstances and subject to a life cycle. Balanced acceptance of interdependence and mortality ends existential dissatisfaction and is the mark of wisdom.

Satipatthāna Sutta: Contemplation of Mental States

The Five Hindrances

And how, monks, does a monk live contemplating mental objects in mental objects?

Herein, monks, a monk lives contemplating mental objects in the mental objects of the five hindrances.

How, monks, does a monk live contemplating mental objects in the mental objects of the five hindrances?

Herein, monks, when sense-desire is present, a monk knows, "There is sense-desire in me," or when sense-desire is not present, he knows, "There is no sense-desire in me." He knows how the arising of the non-arisen sense-desire comes to be; he knows how the abandoning of the arisen sense-desire comes to be; and he knows how the non-arising in the future of the abandoned sense-desire comes to be.

When anger is present, he knows, "There is anger in me," or when anger is not present, he knows, "There is no anger in me." He knows how the arising of the non-arisen anger comes to be; he knows how the abandoning of the arisen anger comes to be; and he knows how the non-arising in the future of the abandoned anger comes to be.

When sloth and torpor are present, he knows, "There are sloth and torpor in me," or when sloth and torpor are not present, he knows, "There are no sloth and torpor in me." He knows how the arising of the non-arisen sloth and torpor comes to be; he knows how the abandoning of the arisen sloth and torpor comes to be; and he knows how the non-arising in the future of the abandoned sloth and torpor comes to be.

When agitation and remorse are present, he knows, "There are agitation and remorse in me," or when agitation and remorse are not present, he knows, "There are no agitation and remorse in me." He knows how the arising of the non-arisen agitation and remorse comes to be; he knows how the abandoning of the arisen agitation and remorse comes to be; and he knows how the non-arising in the future of the abandoned agitation and remorse comes to be.

When doubt is present, he knows, "There is doubt in me," or when doubt is not present, he knows, "There is no doubt in me." He knows how the arising of the non-arisen doubt comes to be; he knows how the abandoning of the arisen doubt comes to be; and he knows how the non-arising in the future of the abandoned doubt comes to be.

Thus he lives contemplating mental objects in mental objects internally, or he lives contemplating mental objects in mental objects externally, or he lives contemplating mental objects in mental objects internally and externally. He lives contemplating origination factors in mental objects, or he lives contemplating dissolution factors in mental objects, or he lives contemplating origination-and-dissolution factors in mental objects. Or his mindfulness is established with the thought, "Mental objects exist," to the extent necessary just for knowledge and mindfulness, and he lives detached, and clings to nothing in the world. Thus also, monks, a monk lives contemplating mental objects in the mental objects of the five hindrances.

The Five Aggregates of Clinging
And further, monks, a monk lives contemplating mental objects in the mental objects of the five aggregates of clinging.

How, monks, does a monk live contemplating mental objects in the mental objects of the five aggregates of clinging? Herein, monks, a monk thinks, "Thus is material form; thus is the arising of material form; and thus is the disappearance of material form. Thus is feeling; thus is the arising of feeling; and thus is the disappearance of feeling. Thus is perception; thus is the arising of perception; and thus is the disappearance of perception. Thus are formations; thus is the arising of formations; and thus is the disappearance of formations. Thus is consciousness; thus is the arising of consciousness; and thus is the disappearance of consciousness."

Thus he lives contemplating mental objects in mental objects internally, or he lives contemplating mental objects in mental objects externally, or he lives contemplating mental objects in mental objects internally and externally. He lives contemplating origination factors in mental objects, or he lives contemplating dissolution factors in mental objects, or he lives contemplating origination-and-dissolution factors in mental objects. Or his mindfulness is established with the thought, "Mental objects exist," to the extent necessary just for knowledge and mindfulness, and he lives detached, and clings to nothing in the world. Thus also, monks, a monk lives contemplating mental objects in the mental objects of the five aggregates of clinging.

The Six Internal and External Sense Bases
And further, monks, a monk lives contemplating mental objects in the mental objects of the six internal and the six external sense-bases.

How, monks, does a monk live contemplating mental objects in the mental objects of the six internal and the six external sense-bases?

Herein, monks, a monk knows the eye and visual forms and the fetter that arises dependent on both (the eye and forms); he knows how the arising of the non-arisen fetter comes to be; he knows how the abandoning of the arisen fetter comes to be; and he knows how the non-arising in the future of the abandoned fetter comes to be.

He knows the ear and sounds ... the nose and smells ... the tongue and flavours ... the body and tactual objects ... the mind and mental objects, and the fetter that arises dependent on both; he knows how the arising of the non-arisen fetter comes to be; he knows how the abandoning of the arisen fetter comes to be; and he knows how the nonarising in the future of the abandoned fetter comes to be. Thus he lives contemplating mental objects in mental objects internally, or he lives contemplating mental objects in mental objects externally, or he lives contemplating mental objects in mental objects internally and externally. He lives contemplating origination factors in mental objects, or he lives contemplating dissolution factors in mental objects, or he lives contemplating origination-and-dissolution factors in mental objects. Or his mindfulness is established with the thought, "Mental objects exist," to the extent necessary just for knowledge and mindfulness, and he lives detached, and clings to nothing in the world. Thus, monks, a monk lives contemplating mental objects in the mental objects of the six internal and the six external sense-bases.

The Seven Factors of Enlightenment

And further, monks, a monk lives contemplating mental objects in the mental objects of the seven factors of enlightenment.

How, monks, does a monk live contemplating mental objects in the mental objects of the seven factors of enlightenment?

Herein, monks, when the enlightenment-factor of mindfulness is present, the monk knows, "The enlightenment-factor of mindfulness is in me," or when the enlightenment-factor of mindfulness is absent, he knows, "The enlightenment-factor of mindfulness is not in me;" and he knows how the arising of the non-arisen enlightenment-factor of mindfulness comes to be; and how perfection in the development of the arisen enlightenment-factor of mindfulness comes to be.

When the enlightenment-factor of the investigation of mental objects is present, the monk knows, "The enlightenment-factor of the investigation of mental objects is in me;" when the enlightenment-factor of the investigation of mental objects is absent, he knows, "The enlightenment-factor of the investigation of mental objects is not in me;" and he knows how the arising of the non-arisen enlightenment-factor of the investigation of mental objects comes to be, and how perfection in the development of the arisen enlightenment-factor of the investigation of mental objects comes to be.

When the enlightenment-factor of energy is present, he knows, "The enlightenment factor of energy is in me;" when the enlightenment-factor of energy is absent, he knows, "The enlightenment-factor of energy is not in me;" and he knows how the arising of the non-arisen enlightenment -factor of energy comes to be, and how perfection in the development of the arisen enlightenment factor of energy comes to be.

When the enlightenment-factor of joy is present, he knows, "The enlightenment factor of joy is in me;" when the enlightenment-factor of joy is absent, he knows, "The enlightenment-factor of joy is not in me;" and he knows how the arising of the non-arisen enlightenment-factor of joy comes to be, and how perfection in the development of the arisen enlightenment-factor of joy comes to be.

When the enlightenment-factor of tranquility is present, he knows, "The enlightenment-factor of tranquility is in me;" when the enlightenment factor of tranquility is absent, he knows, "The enlightenment-factor of tranquility is not in me;" and he knows how the arising of the non-arisen enlightenment-factor of tranquility comes to be, and how perfection in the development of the arisen enlightenment-factor of tranquility comes to be.

When the enlightenment-factor of concentration is present, he knows, "The enlightenment-factor of concentration is in me;" when the enlightenment factor of concentration is absent, he knows, "The enlightenment-factor of concentration is not in me;" and he knows how the arising of the non-arisen enlightenment-factor of concentration comes to be, and how perfection in the development of the arisen enlightenment-factor of concentration comes to be.

When the enlightenment-factor of equanimity is present, he knows, "The enlightenment-factor of equanimity is in me;" when the enlightenment factor of equanimity is absent, he knows, "The enlightenment-factor of equanimity is not in me;" and he knows how the arising of the non-arisen enlightenment-factor of equanimity comes to be, and how perfection in the development of the arisen enlightenment-factor of equanimity comes to be.

Thus he lives contemplating mental objects in mental objects internally, or he lives contemplating mental objects in mental objects externally, or he lives contemplating mental objects in mental objects internally and externally. He lives contemplating origination-factors in mental objects, or he lives contemplating dissolution-factors in mental objects, or he lives contemplating origination-and-dissolution-factors in mental objects. Or his mindfulness is established with the thought, "Mental objects exist," to the extent necessary just for knowledge and mindfulness, and he lives detached, and clings to nothing in the world. Thus, monks, a monk lives contemplating mental objects in the mental objects of the seven factors of enlightenment.

The Four Noble Truths

And further, monks, a monk lives contemplating mental objects in the mental objects of the four noble truths.

How, monks, does a monk live contemplating mental objects in the mental objects of the four noble truths?

Herein, monks, a monk knows, "This is suffering," according to reality; he knows "This is the origin of suffering," according to reality; he knows, "This is the cessation of suffering," according to reality; he knows "This is the road leading to the cessation of suffering," according to reality.

Thus he lives contemplating mental objects in mental objects internally, or he lives contemplating mental objects in mental objects externally, or he lives contemplating mental objects in mental objects internally and externally. He lives contemplating origination-factors in mental objects, or he lives contemplating dissolution-factors in mental objects, or he lives contemplating origination-and-dissolution-factors in mental objects. Or his mindfulness is established with the thought, "Mental objects exist," to the extent necessary *just for knowledge and mindfulness, and he lives detached, and clings to nothing in the world. Thus, monks, a monk lives contemplating mental objects in the mental objects of the four noble truths.*[2]

The Flow of Experience

The fourth of the foundations of attention corresponds to the flow of experiential phenomena. The word *dhamma* is used in nearly all doctrines and religions of Indian origin to refer to the truth, the law, or universal order. In Buddhism, *Dhamma* refers to the Buddha's teachings, or the Buddha's truth. By extension, *dhamma* is also used to refer to mental phenomena or events as being the only reality we have. We must remember that for the Buddha, as well as for other Eastern traditions, this experience is more real than the outside world. The only certainty is what is experienced in each moment.

Although we can direct attention towards specific aspects of experience such as somatic activities, those of feeling or of knowing, all of these are encountered in that flow of phenomena that we call "experience."

Experience includes experiencing its own phenomena. In other words, we can develop knowledge about experience, as occurs with the three previous foundations, or we can live the experience. The fourth foundation of attention deals with phenomenological experience—the contemplation of experience just as it is.

It would seem that consciousness can know itself, but in doing so it generates a "blind spot," a moment of separation that in turn produces the interplay of *nama* and *rupa*, *what knows* and *what is known*. From this perspective there is no dualism—instead, it is one thing that turns upon itself and objectifies and materializes it.

This process that collapses consciousness into matter begins with the development of reception and emission systems between the two aspects of consciousness, thereby producing the appearance of inside-outside. The

---

[2] Our deep gratitude for the translation of "Satipatthāna Sutta: The Foundations of Mindfulness" (MN 10), from the Pali by Nyanasatta Thera. Access to Insight (BCBS Edition), 1 December 2013, http://www.accesstoinsight.org/tipitaka/mn/mn.010.nysa.html.

generation of a limit gives rise to the experience of separation between one and the other. From now on, the maintenance of one is prioritized over the whole, and it becomes the individual.

The centrality and sovereignty of the individual converts the flow of consciousness into an individual experience, a management system based upon receiving and transmitting information. Through this, the individual is able to sustain the experience of existing as a separate entity.

Experience begins with sensation, which is the experience of connecting. Contact involves the object, the receiver, and consciousness. For instance, shape and color are the object that an eye can receive, but this contact would not produce anything were there to be no consciousness. *What knows* the contact between the eye and the visible object is visual awareness. To have visual knowledge or awareness does not mean objective knowledge, in the sense of true knowledge, given that the eye is only able to capture what it has been conditioned for, its materiality being a type of that same conditioning. To have awareness or to be aware does not imply that this is decided voluntarily, even though awareness implies intentionality (as this is materialized in the evolutionary process itself, generating behaviors that are not explicitly elaborated but rather implicitly executed). The remarkable thing about this process is that we can convert what realizes into the object of realization, giving rise to a process of self-knowledge, self-transformation, and self-transcendence.

> **We can convert what realizes into the object of realization, giving rise to a process of self-knowledge, self-transformation, and self-transcendence.**

It is not a case then that the object and the sensory base produce consciousness but that there must be consciousness for the object and the base to make contact. In this model, consciousness is a fundamental component of reality that is beyond space and time. As we saw in the contemplation of the mind, time is a concept that is the origin of the individual, while space is another concept that begins with proprioception and is then represented internally, thereby creating the mental space of representations. Consciousness is what maintains balance. It is needed for material objects and matter in the sensory base to produce sensation by their interaction, which is space-time located experience. The knowing operations performed on sensation generate a personalized perception of the world.

The Five Hindrances

To heed the fourth foundation is to heed the flow of experience and recognize in it the products of conditioning, stripping back experience until its disappearance.

A stable mind is only possible if it transcends a series of limitations that we nevertheless consider to be inherent to its own functioning. Firstly, one must transcend doubt in the form of critical thoughts, which prevent us from immersing ourselves in the natural flow of phenomena—what we have called "first-person experience." Secondly, one must free oneself from preferences and expectations, which come in the shape of, for example, ill will or a desire for sensual pleasures. Thirdly, a stable mind needs to know how to manage skillfully moments of agitation or torpor that occur regularly, whether due to psychodynamic circumstances or organismic causes. These then are the obstacles that the *Sutta* refers to, and we intend to clarify them in this section.

When we practice meditation, we are using a technology that modifies the flow of phenomena. Although we are paying attention to the tactile sensations of breathing or we are listening to outside noise, it is our feelings or thoughts that take on a greater dimension. There is an abundance of incoming information from the mind itself, and not so much from the external senses. As we go deeper into meditation, attention focuses on experience and its most intimate nooks. There is a change of perspective that aims to witness mental phenomena more clearly and to limit the influence of physical phenomena on the process. To be precise, the "meditative set-up" is designed to experience more clearly exactly how the mind constructs experience.

If the psychological system worked properly, we could direct attention towards the respiratory process without any interruption, and we could be present in the whole range of bodily movements and activities. It would not be doubted that the body is nothing more than a set of processes with a life cycle; rather, it would be accepted that the mind makes an experience pleasant or unpleasant, and that the mind constructs concepts and beliefs that pollute the experience and are not healthy for the body.

However, unfortunately, there is a whole series of activities that stops the system from simply paying attention to phenomena as they emerge and cease to be. *Sati* and *samadhi*, well balanced by *vayama*, could repose on the respiratory process (or on any other object or process) the limited unified attention skills capable of effortlessly observing the process moment by moment. However, when we want to turn our attention to the flow of experience, attention fluctuates, and our attention resources wane. To be able to attend consciously, we choose one single process, breathing, which helps us learn *samadhi* or the necessary psychological activity so as to be present in all the experience processes. Whichever process we choose, the mind has to learn to be attentive, focused, and stable. To this end, it has to overcome what the *Sutta* calls "hindrances" to *samadhi*. (See Figure 12.)

The hindrances to *samadhi* are the hindrances of the attention system. *Sati* attends to changes in *samadhi* and *vayama*. *Samadhi* is in charge of directing attentional focus, but it suffers from the hindrances of selective attention—that is to say, the conditioning of what to focus on and how to focus effectively. The amount of effort and activation depends on *vayama*, which suffers from the hindrances of alertness and vigilance—in other words, too much effort or laxness when exercising attention.

This may seem contradictory, but it is a polarity. We tend towards either over-exerting and making too many demands on ourselves, or on the contrary, self-condescension and self-indulgence. In one case, there is an excess of effort, and in the other, an excess of laxity.

Sceptical Doubt (Vicikiccha)	Cognitive Regulation
Sensuous Desire (Kamacchanda)	Emotional Regulation
Ill Will (Uyapada)	
Sloth and Torpor (Thina-Middha)	Physiological Regulation
Restlessness (Udhacca-Kukkucca)	
Hindrances	**Skills**

Figure 12: The obstacles to mental stability and the psychological skills needed to manage them.

Understanding the Hindrances

Although it is traditional to talk of five hindrances, what does this concept really mean? A pedagogical and descriptive way of looking at it is based on three forces employed by "that which realizes" to relate to the phenomenon: *safe-insecure*, *attractive-repulsive*, and *active-inactive*.

The five hindrances can be understood as the flow of experience subject to these three forces. Certainty controls distrust, satisfaction controls desire, and agency controls interest.

The first hindrance is traditionally labelled as "doubt," and it is experienced as cognitive resistance to ceasing its activity. In other words, doubt is thought necessary for adequate cognitive activity. The "I narrator" we have referred to, for instance, tends to get involved continually.

This "I" is a construct with all the conscious and unconscious memories of what it considers "its history." This history is woven from beliefs and expectations about itself, concepts and ideas about things, and judgments and perceptions elaborated to suit itself. It is continuously opining and making decisions based on all of this, believing that it is a sovereign and lasting entity, rational and correct. Every kind of image, memory, and thought emerge in the mind because of its inertia. Doubt is the manifestation in experience of a lower level of certainty, or confidence, held in the practice of conscious attention as a method for liberation.

Affective reactivity is usually described as the obstacle of "desire for sensual pleasures" and "ill will." The conditioned mind tends to seek its usual "sensual palliatives" and to obsess over its preferred "enemies" instead of reposing in serenity. Individual and family survival are the origins of the pursuit of pleasure and avoidance of pain. Attacks, avoidance, sexual desire, caring for oneself and for others, the desire to exist, submission, comparison, and depression are deeply and unconsciously entrenched in the human mind, and they have been modelled in everybody by the search for reinforcement and by the avoidance of frustration. The considerable force of attraction and repulsion has resulted in addictions and aversions that dominate our lives, even if we justify our actions with the very best reasoning and a longing for justice.

Activation-level conditioning ranges between "restlessness or agitation" and "sloth or lethargy." Working together with the other obstacles, the organism gets agitated or depressed, preventing us from being attentive to the present. Regulating the activation level of the organism is a primary function, one that is very primitive and basic. Although it can be affected by abrupt changes in the environment, as well as by voluntary activation or relaxation activities, it has a characteristic tonic shape in each organism. To speak about the activation level is to speak about the vitality of the organism.

The alertness level is the energetic momentum of the organism. Activation is subservient to survival of the individual or species and is directed by the reflexes of orientation and selective attention. Whatever in the immediate environment that may be good or dangerous for the organism is selected. This selection and orientation system starts out as an unconscious orientation reflex, programmed by phylogenetic inheritance and preverbal experiences, which later becomes a conscious skill that helps guide us towards what interests us, or escape from anything that is threatening.

There is also subliminal guidance that works based on prejudice and an ability to inhibit any tendencies that depend on executive attention. Executive attention also needs a sufficient level of activation to be able to

Integral Vipassana

> ***Sati* detects the changes in the quality and content of awareness, not concepts.**

perform its functions. Too much activation starts up automatic processing, potentially resulting in more errors; too low an activation level does not allow us to clearly detect what the mind is doing, and consequently, we're unable to execute actions which are appropriate to the situation. When both intention and selection cease, alertness always remains as passive surveillance. It will only kickstart the other two systems when there is a real danger to the survival of the organism.

Notwithstanding, the labels used to name obstacles can confuse us. *Sati* detects the changes in the quality and content of awareness, not concepts. It is not particularly useful to observe the obstacles' content in itself, which is often times obvious and repetitive. What *is* useful is the change resulting from the interference by the other attentional networks that drag observation towards other phenomena. These interferences can be changes in the activation level of the organism and a resulting oscillation between agitation and lethargy. There can also be cognitive changes that oscillate between uncertainty and credulity, and above all, affective obstacles that oscillate between attraction and repulsion.

So, attention is subject to opposing forces that mutually cancel out at the point of equilibrium: calmness for the level of activation, confidence for the cognitive, and impartiality for the affective.

Maintaining Balance in the Face of Hindrances

The "meditative stage" modifies the usual state of consciousness. The body is used to responding to external and internal stimuli with physical or verbal behavior. However, in meditative practice behavior is restricted by immobility and silence, which in turn produces physical tension or mental agitation. This tension can grow because of the effort of focusing attention on the phenomenon (*samadhi*) and the agitation due to the high speed of the process, which stops us from being present in the changes (*sati*).

Vayama is in charge of maintaining balance or, to put it another way, of managing the tension and agitation. Too much effort on concentration leads to mental irritation and obsession, while too much attention to change produces disorientation and confusion.

To be present in the process, or *sati*, is to keep processing slowly, frame by frame. Reducing processing speed allows for an improved focus on each phenomenon (*samadhi*). Improved focus makes it more obvious when there is presence, which then allows us to realize there is change in the phenomenon. At first, *sati* often is lost due to the intrusion of a conditioned phenomenon—and when it reappears, many phenomena may have passed without us detecting them. However, with training we can be present when the new phenomenon arises, and in time we can be present at the beginning, middle, and end of the entire sequence without obsessing or becoming disorientated.

When we deliberately try to pay attention to the process of mental phenomena, we discover that most of the time, *sati* is not present. Instead, the experience process is being controlled by a series of automated associative chains, composed of cognitive prejudices, affective preferences, and alterations in the level of body alertness. If our only intention is to keep focusing on a single object, we will not realize that all this activity is going on, and we will continue voluntarily stretching the system without understanding precisely how it works. However, if the intention is to discover how dissatisfaction works, we will see that the process has its own dynamics, and the illusion that "I" controls the experience will begin to fade.

The change in the body's activation level imposed by being both immobile and vertical may produce pleasure or displeasure. These in turn may be related to sensory images or memories that activate or deactivate the organism in a continuous chain of associations and modifications that the "I" in its usual state of consciousness may not even notice. Those are the manifestation of the "hindrances." The mind, explicitly or implicitly, realizes that there are continual changes in the object of attention and begins to experience the strength of the interconnections, which stops it from breaking and stopping them. The development of *sati* will reveal these conditionings, bringing about effective regulation of the incoming information by the six senses, its affective evaluation, and its cognitive processing.

Integral Vipassana

Staying Connected with Sati

Sati is lost when any of these chains fires up, and it reappears when its strength equals that of the connection linking the chain. At first, when *sati* returns at the end of an associative chain, it does so to fulfill its original intention—that is, to pay attention to the mental phenomena in progress without being carried away by the associations. When it reappears, *sati* can resume its work with whatever occupied the foreground of the experience, or if it does not know how or when it disconnected, it can return to the object of meditation, which is the safest way to know that it is reconnected.

The recourse to the meditation object has the function of "a safe house" with which we can re-establish conscious attention and strengthen focused attention (*samadhi*). As we have seen, it is a good idea to start out by focusing on physical objects such as breathing or body postures until you are able to discriminate between the physical and the mental phenomena (*namarupa*). With practice, *sati* can be present at the beginning of the chain and even stop it before it starts up, or it can remain active throughout the process of appearance and disappearance of any other process.

First you learn to recognize the presence or absence of *sati*, which is the difference between conscious attention and being on "autopilot." Second, you learn not to voluntarily intervene in the respiratory process (suspension of executive functions). Finally, you learn to cultivate the preference for the breathing process over other somatic experiences (suspension of sensory affective habits).

Sati becomes lost, and when it reappears it encounters thoughts. If it heeds these thoughts, it will see a recurring theme of the mind that, having gained enough momentum, may be sufficiently strong to again push *sati* aside and continue thinking about that very same subject. Until *sati* detects the force of attraction or repulsion that has led it to that type of thinking, this will be repeated ad infinitum. *Sati* is lost and discovers that there is desire for something. If the force of attraction has grown enough and is stronger than *sati*, it ends up by believing that it is a necessity or it surrenders to the fantasy of desire. *Sati* disappears and appears in a perturbing rage that produces physical sensations categorized as unpleasant, which then leads to *sati* being lost again and agitation growing ever stronger.

Sati disappears and a proliferation of thoughts arise, causing the body to become unbalanced. This agitation is stronger than *sati* and drags the process into wondering why this has happened, which in turn produces more agitation in a negative feedback loop that leads to fear and panic.

You can reinduce calm by paying attention to the object, but if there is no conscious attention at the start of this storm of thoughts, this equilibrium is lost again and again.

Sati can also get lost in a state of drowsiness—which, if sufficiently strong, generates thoughts about the need to rest, or about how boring the situation is—or it can get lost in a kind of cloud where nothing is clearly observed.

Pain can also be a culprit. If it's stronger than *sati* when it appears in the body, pain sets off a storm of thoughts and justifications that cause an emotional fear reaction followed by catastrophic thoughts. The other potential result of pain is that immobility is abandoned. Pain appears in the body and a proliferation of pleasant thoughts or images try to trick the mind, but instead there is an internal struggle that perturbs, and you end up reacting with a change of posture, an action that strengthens the pattern of avoiding discomfort or dissatisfaction.

When *sati* is strong, however, we can look into the character of pain and discover that it is changeable. We see that pain originates from a physical sensation that has been categorized as unpleasant. It can be experienced externally—not as something personal, but rather as a series of mental activities that add to the physical sensation. If *sati* is maintained, and we're able to recognize the impermanence and impersonality of pain, dissatisfaction is limited to a series of fleeting experiences that do not unbalance the mind.

> **If *sati* is maintained, and we're able to recognize the impermanence and impersonality of pain, dissatisfaction is limited to a series of fleeting experiences that do not unbalance the mind.**

A whole range of interactions among the hindrances arise in the absence of *sati*. As they are common experiences, we tend to believe they are real. However, the truth is that they are conditioned affective reactive patterns, routine responses to important situations. Here, the change of register—from the cognitive to the affective, from the cognitive to the bodily, from the bodily to the affective, etc.—is an endless cycle.

For instance, repression begins with a classic conditioning where an idea or image takes on a negative value because it is associated with too strong an activation. In a second phase, repression happens when an idea or fantasy that has acquired a negative value is avoided and kept far from attention—an avoidance behavior that has started to use the fast-processing schema.

Working with the Hindrances

Of the three types of hindrances, the affective are the strongest, those of activation are the most profound, and the cognitive are the most insidious. Cognitive hindrances are the "I" wanting to run the operation, but the "I" is fed by the strength of desire which manifests itself in affective hindrances. The organism has a primary impulse that emerged as it evolved, something that we share with most animals that makes us seek out what we like and avoid what we dislike. This impulse has been conditioned by a history of reinforcement, the result of which is character. So the affective dimension or record is what is mainly in charge of maintaining the illusion of an "I" directing operations. The affective obstacles draw their energy from those of activation. The activation thresholds set the energy environment where the other two move.

> **The simple presence of *sati* allows for liberating changes in the mental process, better known as insights.**

Working with hindrances is the therapeutic part of modern mindfulness, in so much as it deals with deconditioning the "I." By spending more time in the step-by-step processing style that characterizes *sati*, we can access much information that was hidden by rapid processing and reactive chains. The organism learns better when it focuses better and is working at an activation level appropriate to the task. This modifies many of the processes and mechanisms that generated suffering. The simple presence of *sati* allows for liberating changes in the mental process, better known as insights.

Insights are small or big discoveries, though it might be better to call them "rediscoveries," as mostly they are things that were known before but are now forgotten. A typical example is a trauma that may have been repressed because it is just too painful or hard to process, but that, under certain conditions, may return to consciousness. The price paid for forgetting might be a symptom, an inhibition, or a depression, though these symptoms can disappear if our mind manages to remember and restructure itself.

A *lapsus*, or failing to carry out an action, is another example of "forgetting." Somebody who does not want to make a particular phone call "forgets" to do it, or it only comes to mind when it is impossible to make the call. Or perhaps, for the sake of security, this person does not answer any calls at all, even those unconnected with the unpleasant phone call they should make. Or, whenever they remember they should make that call, they decide to deal with another matter beforehand and afterwards they no longer remember there is a phone call to make.

Sati may disappear for a few moments and then reappear after a certain time has elapsed, and it is remembered as something that arose that was identified with and then lost. Somehow, the "I" became involved and *sati* disappeared. When the "I" gets involved, all its memories are involved too, and *sati*, which is attention to the present moment, disappears—engulfed by memories and plans.

> **To feel victimized by the past is to wish that certain things never happened, an impossible wish.**

When the mind projects into the future or the past, it is trapped by insecurity or melancholy. To feel victimized by the past is to wish that certain things never happened, an impossible wish. To project oneself into the future is to venture into an area of uncertainty. Sadness is the emotional mark of the past, anxiety that of the future.

If the hindrance is stronger than *sati*, what has been glimpsed is once again hidden among all the morass of activities that personalize and relocate what we see. If *sati* is strong, the vision lasts long enough for it to be registered, which changes the relationship of forces. If *sati* is lost and there is a decision to return to the primary object, the chain is also cut and there is an unconscious benefit. In any case, we have intervened in the process from a position that transforms it. In both cases the situation created is new and, therefore, this increases the repertoire, the experience of freedom and creativity.

The present is a workspace where many things happen, and *sati* trains to sustain itself in the working memory space. When there is *sati*, the activities that are being processed at the moment can be monitored. *Sati* can take into account any changes in the activation of the organism, it can recognize forces of attraction or repulsion towards the phenomenon in transit, it can label the type of phenomenon (as well as its trigger), etc. Thus, we have a broad but precise monitoring, a new pattern in that data that generates an insight—all without mixing in will or intention. That's why it is called an insight—it is intuitive knowledge that does not undergo any rational analysis.

Non-Attentive Activity and Sati

Sati is an attentional activity and therefore a "top-down" regulatory activity of the somatic, affective, and cognitive registers. However, not all "top-down" processes must necessarily be initiated in an "attentive" fashion. Many emotional or affective responses originate in an unconscious evaluation of the stimulus coming from the executive attention itself, based on expectations, beliefs, or values. In other words, they are significant elements for the person that have become automated according to their semantic value and not just the strength of connection. They are patterns that arise from automating routines.

When we undertake a new task, we consciously pay attention to all the steps, but when the task is repeated over and over again, there is no longer any need to be aware of all the steps—the task becomes automated. This allows us to free up our limited attention resources to learn new tasks or to supervise automated ones. It is the difference between what we previously called "automatic processing," "implicit," "non-attentional," and what we called "controlled processing," "explicit," or "attentional." As we have seen, there are many reactions that do not undergo this process. They have become automated due to types of conditioning, and are activated depending on the connection strength. Nevertheless, they went from being conscious to unconscious by dint of repetition, and their link is more semantic than procedural.

> **Despite our conviction that we are rational beings, our ultimate motivations are determined by feelings.**

Once the task is automated, it basically becomes an autonomous response pattern. If it starts up, it cannot be stopped, and, logically, it cannot adapt to change. Thus, automatic processing is much faster and saves conscious processing a lot of effort, but the latter can function step by step and so is able to change tack on each step. What is more, conscious processing is greatly influenced by cultural and social considerations of what is right or wrong, and these largely determine behavior.

Liberation from Hindrances

To sum up, the mind is a complicated network of automated response patterns that originate in a primitive affective judgment (*vedana*) that began as a survival tool at some point in the evolutionary process. It is modulated by individual experience and conditioned by cultural and social values and norms. The emotional field is what controls our lives without our being aware of it. Despite our conviction that we are rational beings, our ultimate motivations are determined by feelings.

When we have to make a decision, we experience a feeling, while simultaneously imagining a possible solution. This feeling affects the body, and the bodily reaction affects the imagined solution. This mechanism, which has been called a *somatic marker* (Antonio Damasio), generates automatic affective knowledge that allows us to take decisions without conscious knowledge of all the possibilities and their consequences.

Liberation from hindrances makes the mind less clinging and more flexible. However, being carried away by hindrances, no matter how personal they may appear, leads to agitation, desire, and a proliferation of thoughts or mental representations, thereby making an experience unsatisfactory.

By understanding that those tendencies that seemed to be protection systems are precisely the obstacles that prevent calm of the body and mind, calm is restored and the obstacles tend to disappear.

The importance of *samadhi* lies in the understanding that the system works better, and the experience is more joyful, when activity and energy are balanced. This balance depends, to a great degree, on the tranquility generated by not rejecting or attacking activities that are experienced very deeply. Doing so would impede coherence between the components of the system.

It goes without saying that clinging and retaining are equally destabilizing tendencies that may become immensely strong, but if the objectives are considered adaptive because they produce physical or mental pleasure, or because they are in harmony with the physical and mental surroundings, the mind considers them less threatening. Ultimately, ethics consists of deciding on the right thing to do, of taking sides. Doing the right thing balances *vayama* and produces *samadhi*.

In brief, hindrances are cognitive and affective activities that impact the body. The attention management that occurs as an effect of working on hindrances has a vital role to play in regulating the body, which is why results have been obtained in emotional regulation, body awareness, and self-awareness through mindfulness.

Regulating all these activities makes the experience less dominated by the forces of attraction and repulsion, agitation, and drowsiness, as well as images and thoughts. When *sati* spends more time accompanying the experience process, the experience is deeper and more fluid and relaxed—that is to say, there is more *samadhi* and also more *vayama*. However, it can also lead to an impression of achievement that strengthens the supposed "I."

Freedom from obstacles deepens *samadhi*, and there will come a moment when the observer and the observed merge into *jhana*. Should you arrive at this point accompanied by *sati*, you will understand the impermanence, dissatisfactions, and impersonality of physical and mental phenomena. You also will understand that, in experience, there is only mind and matter emerging and disappearing.

As it is understood today, one cannot achieve the psychotherapeutic potential of mindfulness if obstacles are seen as negative aspects to be eliminated. In meditation, we do not reflect on the contents of what appears, but rather act on the strength of the connection that binds it.

> **In meditation, we do not reflect on the contents of what appears, but rather act on the strength of the connection that binds it.**

There is no interpretation, and therefore it is not usual psychotherapy. The achievement is that the organismic activity is at rest thanks to the deactivation of the conditioned associative chains that produce agitation, depression, or worry. Contemplation does not go into the reason for these associations, nor does it search out causes or try to find logical inconsistencies. It is not interested in the underlying cognitive schema. However, by deactivating connections and understanding significant causal relationships between the content, it may be that some contents reappear outside the "meditation stage," where the meditator may become distracted by trying to interpret or modify them. Many times, the meditator stops contemplating and instead plays the game of reflection or interpretation.

Through developing *sati* and learning how to be fully present in the flow of experience, Vipassana meditation demonstrates when and how value judgment, reflection, or interpretation impede full attention, thereby generating dissatisfaction. These activities may seem "noble" to us, but they are based on the belief in an "I." Mindfulness can reach a deeper

Integral Vipassana

dimension if you understand the importance of the force that binds the mind to obstacles, whether by the strength of connection or of meaning, although even in that case it could still be misused as a tool for strengthening the "self" and not for its transcendence.

The natural flow of experience has to do with internal cohesion and not with society's dominant values or social norms. Freedom is not always well understood in a society that wants idols who meet their expectations of perfection. Internal coherence does not necessarily have to correspond to the personal expectation of what a "realized person" is. The belief is that realized people will be at the service of others with an unimpeachable attitude, but this has more to do with each individual's "ideal self" and with the expectation of perfection "for me," rather than with the "ideal of I," which would be what there is of interest in the other person for me to develop "in myself."

Internal coherence is the experience of the arising and ceasing of all phenomena and takes *sati* as its precursor. The practice of concentration (*samadhi*) takes one phenomenon at a time, thereby producing mental calm or *samatha*. Although the collapse of the mind's activity in *jhana* can be caused by fixing attention (*samadhi*) or by being present in the entire breathing process (*sati*), Vipassana prefers to continue to cultivate *sati* rather than the ecstatic experience of *samadhi*—hence the epithets of "dry insight" and "wet insight."

> **Transcendence occurs when *sati* attends to a mind freed from desire.**

When there are no hindrances to heeding the emergence and cessation of physical and mental phenomena, one of the three characteristics of existence presents itself more clearly. If you have discovered the emergence and cessation of physical sensations, you become a master of impermanence. If you discover emergence and cessation in the game of desire, you become a master of dissatisfaction. If you discover the emergence and cessation of ideas, concepts, and perspectives, you become a master of impersonality.

Ultimately, *sati* allows the organism to function at a tonic alert level that facilitates learning and understanding. Through *sati*, the organism learns that it is perishable, that it is moved by the pursuit of pleasure and the avoidance of pain, and that it can unlearn that programming. In this way, the mind can access a state that does not depend on external circumstances. It is free from attachment to things and ideas, but not free from the desire to exist.

Sati and Transcendence

Sati reveals the interdependence of physical, affective, and cognitive phenomena, and hence the absence of a permanent entity that directs the experience process. In the first three foundations of attention as described in the *Sutta*, there is a point where that understanding begins the process of transcendence of "itself." Transcendence occurs when *sati* is present in the dissolution of the somatic experience into its fundamental qualities, and it is understood that a human being is nothing more than the temporary association of elements that will eventually end up separating with the decomposition of the body.

Transcendence occurs when *sati* witnesses a feeling of well-being that does not depend on the body. It occurs when *sati* attends to a mind freed from desire. It occurs when *sati* can be present in the emergence and cessation of all phenomena. Finally, transcendence occurs when it is no longer possible to believe in an "I"—when we recognize that there is nothing except those very same activities all heaped up and mixed up: somatic experience, affective experience, perceptual experience, cognitive experience, and the awareness of experience.

Modern mindfulness develops observation skills of the self in a neutral way, almost as if it were not "me." This technique works very well because it gives an "outsider" perspective on experience and induces a certain calmness. Mindfulness strengthens the knowledge of "oneself." Its

> **Vipassana is the understanding of how the illusion of any "I" is created.**

Integral Vipassana

psychological utility is undeniable, but it does not necessarily lead to transpersonal or spiritual development.

This neutral observer is still a new version of the "I" (albeit smaller and less neurotic), one based on the belief that it is "I" who meditates. However, the objective of Vipassana meditation is not to create a new "meditator I" but rather *to see through the illusion of this "I."* Vipassana is the understanding of how the illusion of any "I" is created.

The so-called observer trap is transcended if the witness is unmasked. Although the first step is to become a witness to the experience, the second is to realize that "I am not the witness." To be able to take this step, the *Sutta* proposes these following three steps: the aggregates, the sense spheres, and the awakening factors.

Without hindrances, the top-down activities have been reduced to an alert presence that heeds processes it no longer identifies with. The top-down activities do not hide the bottom-up activities. A series of psychophysiological processes emerge and cease continuously without the need for anybody to oversee them. Even if the understanding of this emergence and cessation of all phenomena loosens the clinging grip on the "self," the desire to exist forces the observer to continue to take refuge in the aggregate activities that make up a human being—somatic experience, desire, perception, mental formations, and the ability to know.

Sati is in somatic experience, but it is not *the* somatic experience. Experiences such as "I am the body," "I have a body," "This is my body," or "I am in this body" are ways in which the "self" clings to existence by identifying with the "body," even though the body is not the "self." Neither is the "self" in feelings (even if there are feelings), nor is it in perception or the other knowing activities (even if there is perception and other activities that permit knowing). These aggregates are conditioned, impermanent, impersonal, and unsatisfactory activities, but they are the last bastion of the possibility of being something or of being someone, which is why they are often called *attachment aggregates*, attachments to existence. The "I" will try to identify with any of the aggregates with the sole objective of continuing to exist as body, desire, perception, mental patterns, or consciousness.

To no longer exist is not easy. The phenomenology that accompanies this process cannot be said to be ecstatic and wonderful. What is considered reality dissolves just as soon as it appears. The very feeling of "I" disappears. Somatic experience disappears, and then any other object of consciousness. All seems vague and dark. There is a feeling of fear about disappearance. Neuralgic pain may occur, tears for the loss of loved ones. There is fear of everything. The game of physical sensations and mental activities (*namarupa*), which used to be fun, is now insubstantial. There is no feeling of pleasure or joy. Although all of this does happen, there is also no experience of feeling trapped by all this phenomenology.

The very experience of inhaling and exhaling disappears. There is a feeling of irritation due to the appearances and disappearances of all physical and mental experience. The understanding of impermanence, dissatisfaction, and no-self sharpens.

Everything is experienced as boring or ugly. Laziness floods the experience. A profound sadness accompanies the experience of separation from everything that is loved. If before there was an experience of boredom, now boredom is everything. There is nothing left to enjoy or anything that you want to know. Neither fame nor fortune interest. Everything is viewed as decaying and decadent. Old age, disease, and death prevail. At the same time all this is happening, there comes a grim determination to continue until an exit can be found.

During meditation one can feel itching and biting, as if the whole body were covered in insects. Impatience arises and there is no way to feel comfortable. Then come desires to abandon meditation, to abandon this path. You can convince yourself that you are not ready. You can experience stiffness, heaviness, burning, and other worrying sensations, but they disappear at the same speed that they arrive.

Finally, you stop feeling scared, but neither are you happy. A feeling of calm overwhelms. The mind becomes peaceful and subdued for quite some time. In fact, time ceases to exist. The calm becomes stable. The experience is easy and the body regenerates. It is understood that there is nothing to cling to.

Awareness Without Object

The subject begins to emerge from the somatic experience that gives rise to the "proto-I," a primitive awareness of individuality whose sole purpose is to stay alive. When the ability to learn based on the evaluation or the assessment of somatic experience was added to that, a "nuclear self" emerged that reacted to contacts, in real time, for adaptive purposes. When this nuclear self "time-travelled" through the understanding of causation and remembered some previous contact, it was able to choose the reaction based on a planned future, which is when the "autobiographical self" appeared.

Seeing that there was continuity and that it could react or not react depending on the situation, it believed itself to be an autonomous and separate being—and that condemned it to be incomplete. Now the problem is how to escape from that dissatisfaction. To achieve this, you have to return along the same path to remember how you got into that situation in the first place—all the while knowing that what has been developed will still be there, even if it is neither truth nor reality.

Sati functions as a thread of attention that has witnessed the fading of ordinary or conventional reality. It has pursued any form of identification—even in those activities that generate awareness—and has experienced that to exist it must be aware of something, even if it is awareness of self.

To reveal the mystery, *sati* has to go before awareness makes contact with itself, and the only way to do this is to go where consciousness of something arises. It has to penetrate experience to where phenomena originate, the contact between the sensory bases and their objects. As we have seen, this contact or sensation arises from the meeting between the stimulus, the sensory organ, and consciousness. If this contact does not occur, there is no awareness of something—all the phenomena that it has witnessed.

Latent Tendencies

Contemplation takes place in the six sensory bases that disguise the "latent tendencies," which are the primary programming of the psychophysical organism. Remarkably, affective neuroscience has discovered seven primary processes buried in ancient subcortical areas of all mammalian brains, and if we apply them to the Buddha's *Dhamma* model, they correspond with those "latent tendencies." The eradication of these tendencies is, according to this model, what puts an end to dissatisfaction.

The latent tendencies reside in the consciousness of the six senses—visual, auditory, olfactory, taste, tactile, and mental awareness. It is as if each of these sensory doorways has a mind that is conditioned to remain dormant until something knocks on their door. These tendencies are desire, aversion, comparison, an erroneous view or belief in the existence of the self, the desire to exist, uncertainty, and ignorance.

> There is no possibility of advancing because the awareness of nothingness is nothing but awareness. Vipassana ends here.

First, the belief in the existence of an "I" that manages the whole process is abandoned, and that ends any lingering doubt about the usefulness of the method. Then, the forces of attraction and repulsion that keep us tied to things—and later those that keep us tied to ideas, concepts, and perception—are all weakened. Lastly, we stop comparing and differentiating ourselves, and give up the desire to exist. Serenity invades every last corner of the "body/mind." This leads us to the ultimate that can be known—and that is wisdom.

The understanding of the activity of these six spheres of the senses leads us to the very moment before sensation, to the moment before any of the six consciences come to meet their object. In other words, to the point where awareness takes no object, not even itself. When consciousness is not consciousness of anything, it is only infinite consciousness, emptiness. This is the end of the illusion.

Integral Vipassana

Characteristics of Empty Awareness

Sati has completed its journey. There is no possibility of advancing because the awareness of nothingness is nothing but awareness. Vipassana ends here.

At this point, *sati* becomes the basis of discernment, energy, joy, tranquility, non-duality, and equanimity—the factors that lead to *nibbana*. It is the beginning of a new path where *sati* has no function but is the reference, in this case negative, of whether or not there is *nibbana*.

Once the illusion has faded, the body/mind can continue to play with sensations, desires, and knowledge. *Conscious attention means that nothing is sought out, precisely because it is understood that there is nothing to seek.* It plays at putting itself in different perspectives; it is powerful without being arrogant; it is happy because nothing can deceive and sadden it; it is calm because it knows how to take care of itself; it is not afraid; it is not divided between being or not being; it has no preferences. Thus, it is satisfied. Constant conscious attention is the hallmark of wisdom.

Understanding of Truth

In our normal state, the "I" is an undoubted experience as well as a social and linguistic necessity. Nobody normally thinks "I am not me." However, systematic contemplation (*sati*) of physical and mental phenomena reveals evidence that there is no such thing we can identify as "I." (See Figure 13.)

There is a biological organism that functions by itself, but many other organisms that do not hold this belief in the "I" function perfectly well. This biological organism is one of continuous transformation, constantly changing its physical makeup and subject to a cycle of birth and death. It is endowed—as a survival resource that arose during the conditioning process—with an activation system and another evaluation system that works autonomously.

The responses of the body/mind to biological and environmental requirements mutate into habits and reactions that trigger without any conscious intervention. Even when there is a *conscious will*, the response is contextual. Among the functions the body/mind uses to know things is what we call intention or will. This is just another function that does

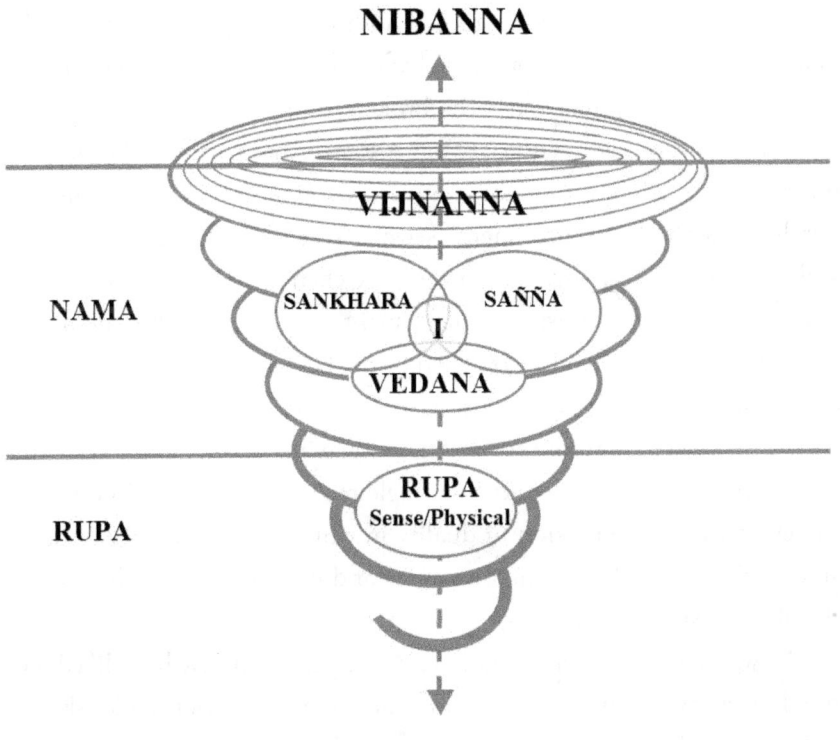

Figure 13: The illusion of "I" arises from activity by the Five Aggregates.

not control all physiological, affective, or cognitive aspects, and cannot therefore be considered to be a stable and permanent entity, but rather an ongoing activity. Experience is the result of all these activities, but with its contemplation comes the dissolution of the separation between the observer and the observed, thus becoming an impersonal experience. Contemplation of experience induces the dissolution of the border between *what knows* and *what is known*—the matrix of experience. *What knows* can expand until it disappears into the immense eternal void, but the material organism will also expand and disintegrate into its composite elements. Travelling the path of *sati* does not lead to discovering a self, essence, or soul in the body or the mind. Rather, it leads to the opposite discovery—that no such self has ever existed. Nothing remains.

Any experience or phenomenon is nothing more than the dizzying play of interdependence between *nama* and *rupa*. Therefore, the idea of centrality and sovereignty of the "I" has been broken.

The "I," then, is not the central instance that controls the process, but rather the attempt to make it understandable or reasonable. Interdependence with the environment is what actually controls our actions and reactions. We can aspire to manage the changes to ensure that they do not perpetuate or increase unhealthy mental states, but the same understanding of good and bad is governed by the belief in the "I." The idea that *what knows* and *what is known* are separate entities has been broken, and with it the idea of limit or separation between inside and outside. By being irreducible, the dualities point to a single reality which turns in on itself, thereby creating the illusion of duality in which the "I" is placed on one side or the other, depending on causes and conditions, thereby missing the global vision—unity.

Now, reflect upon what you have read so far. You may have liked it or not. It may have seemed more or less reasonable to you. But obviously, it is not the complete truth. It is a series of words used to convey a few pieces of knowledge about Buddhism, a few ideas about psychology, and a few neuroscientific hypotheses—all organized in such a way that they follow a script that in turn was pre-established by a mythical story that was written and rewritten over thousands of years. Truth must be more than this.

Real truth lies in experience and in the end of experience. Only there can we understand why we (along with most animals that have a life cycle) suffer and depend on the exterior to find fulfillment. We therefore know that existential anguish can only cease when we accept interdependence and mortality—when the path has been travelled, truth realized, and wisdom achieved.

Satipaṭṭhāna Sutta: Conclusion

Verily, monks, whosoever practices these four foundations of mindfulness in this manner for seven years, then one of these two fruits may be expected by him: highest knowledge (arahantship) here and now, or if some remainder of clinging is yet present, the state of non-returning.

O monks, let alone seven years. Should any person practice these four foundations of mindfulness in this manner for six years... five years... four years... three years... two years... one year, then one of these two fruits may be expected by him: highest knowledge here and now, or if some remainder of clinging is yet present, the state of non-returning.

O monks, let alone a year. Should any person practice these four foundations of mindfulness in this manner for seven months... six months... five months... four months... three months... two months... a month... half a month, then one of these two fruits may be expected by him: highest knowledge here and now, or if some remainder of clinging is yet present, the state of non-returning.

O monks, let alone half a month. Should any person practice these four foundations of mindfulness in this manner for a week, then one of these two fruits may be expected by him: highest knowledge here and now, or if some remainder of clinging is yet present, the state of non-returning.

Because of this it was said: "This is the only way, monks, for the purification of beings, for the overcoming of sorrow and lamentation, for the destruction of suffering and grief, for reaching the right path, for the attainment of Nibbāna, namely the four foundations of mindfulness."

Thus spoke the Blessed One. Satisfied, the monks approved of his words.

(MN 10: Satipaṭṭhāna Sutta; I 55–63)

Sati is constant, balanced, and efficient mindfulness. In other words, it is free from preferences, effortless, and oriented towards health and wellbeing.

Sati is executive awareness capable of directing or inhibiting the focus of attention and of managing the level of tonic alertness.

When supported by precise *samadhi* and adequate *vayama*, *sati* is the activity that allows the mind to integrate and transcend its own activity. These three elements constitute a constant and relaxed conscious attention, which allows for psychological maturation and spiritual awakening.

Through *sati* we can contemplate all those activities that make us human beings. This leads to transformation, allowing us to change so that we may live more satisfactorily.

Vipassana meditation—understood here as the cultivation of the three elements of *Samadhi* (*sati*, *samadhi*, *vayama*) of the Noble Eightfold Path—has therapeutic effects and leads us to self-realization.

Using the *Satipatthāna Sutta* as a guide, we realize that meditation is more than just a method to increase our physical and mental health—ultimately, it supervises the maturation process towards self-transcendence. Training in the four foundations of attention reveals the truth of human existence and helps to release our attachment to it. Transcending individual existence frees us from dissatisfaction.

Training the alertness or surveillance system to contemplate affective and cognitive conditioning without reacting may take more or less time and dedication, depending on many internal and external factors both individual and collective.

But the method brings benefits from the very beginning. It develops relaxation, concentration, emotional regulation, self-acceptance, and creativity. Insight, perseverance, enthusiasm, self-care, confidence, and an absence of credulity are internal factors that can help facilitate this journey, and certain external conditions and sociocultural circumstances can also play a role. Without pausing or forcing oneself, this is the "middle way," the direct path to wisdom.

INDEX

Page numbers followed by *f* indicate figures.

A
Abhidhamma Pitaka, 9–10, 19–21, 106–108, 139
absolute threshold, 73
absorption states, 16–18
acquired affective reactions, 84–86
affective hindrances, 163–166, 168, 170–172
affective reactions, 84–86
affective states, immeasurable, 103–104
Afghanistan, 9–10
Agamas, 20
aggregates, attachment, 176–177, *see also* Five Aggregates of clinging
agitation, 153, 162*f*, 163
Ajahn (term), 14
Ananda, 34
anapanasati (attention to breath), 63–68, 63*f*

Anapanasati Sutta, 64
anatta (non-self), 12, 25*f*, 45, 126, 177
Ancient Greece, 5–6
anger, 153
Anguttara Nikaya, v, 20, 105
anicca (impermanence), 12, 25*f*, 45
appana samadhi (fixed concentration), 17
apparent, conventional, or compound reality *(paññati)*, 113, 124
Arada Kamala, 63–64
Ashoka, 6, 9, 14*f*, 22
attachment *(upadana)*, 86–87, 89–90
attachment aggregates, 176–177, *see also* Five Aggregates of clinging
attention
    basic, 122–123
    to breath *(anapanasati)*, 63–68, 63*f*
    complete, 123
    conditional, 36
    conscious, 180, *see also sati*

Integral Vipassana

focused, *see samadhi*
foundations of, 25, 25f, 30–31, 36, 110
meta-attentional practices, 59
with object, xviiif
in psychology, 131
ten stages of *Kamalashila*, 60, 60f
without object, xviiif
attention networks, xx–xxi, 25f, 34f, 35f, 36, 41–42
atthapaññatti ("thing concept"), 134
autobiographical self, 178
automatic processing, 37–38, 171
Avesta, 6
awakening, xviiif, 18, 25, 150–152
awakening factors, 176
awareness
    citta building blocks of, 112–116
    conscious, 29–47
    empty, 180
    visual awareness (*cakkuviññana*), 111, 159
    without object, 178–179

B

balance, 74, 164–165, 172
ballistic movements, 98–99
behavior(s), 131
    ethical, 144–145
    learned, 82, 97
bhavana (mental training), 59, 114, 127
bhavanga, 129, 139
Bhikkhu Bodhi, 14, 14f
Bible, 6
biological inheritance, 82
"bottom-up" processes, 25, 30, 41–42, 117
Brach, Tara, xxii

Brahmanism, 4
Brahmins, 6
breath and breathing, 26
    attention to breath (*anapanasati*), 63–68, 63f
    mindfulness of breathing, 52–53
Buddha, xiv, 4–5, 14f, 15–16
    speeches, *see* speeches (*Sutta Pitaka*)
    teachings, *see* Pali Canon (*Tipitaka*)
Buddhaghosa, 7, 14f
Buddhahood, 12
Buddhism, 13
    councils, 7–12, 14, 14f
    early, 19–21
    history of, 4–6, 10, 14f
    spread of, 10
Burma, 9–10, 12

C

cakkuviññana (visual awareness), 111
Cambodia, 12
carnal sensations, 92
cause and effect, 95–97
Central Asia, 9
cetana (intention), 135
cetasikas (mental factors), 83, 108, 114–116, 116f, 124–125, 130, 135
Cha, 14
character building, 88, 89f
China, 5, 9–10
Christianity, 5–6
citta (cognitive activity), 106–116, 124–125, 129–130, 135
    characteristics of a free mind, 146–148
    healthy, 115–116, 115f, 123
    process and concepts, 117–119

Index

clinging, *see* Five Aggregates of clinging
cognition(s), 46
    basic processes *(cetasikas)*, 83, 108, 114–116, 116*f*, 131
    as conditioned activity, 119–122
    feelings as cognitive activity, 79–80
    healthy processes, 115–116, 115*f*
    sati as cognitive activity, 122–124
cognitive defusion, xv
cognitive hindrances, 164–165, 168, 170–172
cognitive neuroscience, xxii
compassion meditation, 26
composite phenomena, 124–125
composure, 115–116
concentration, 33
concentration meditation, *see* Samatha meditation
conditional attention, 36
conditioning, 92, 97–101, 150
    of cognitive activity, 119–122
    conditioned realities *(sankharas)*, 112, 124–125
    evaluative, 99
    operant, 99
Confucianism, 5–6
conscious attention, 180, *see also sati*
conscious awareness, 29–47
consciousness
    characteristics of a free mind, 146–148
    contemplation of, 109–110
    mental consciousness *(viññana)*, 111, 135
    mind consciousness *(manoviññana)*, 111
    pre-consciousness, 44
    states of, 25
    structure of, 114, 115*f*
conscious processing, 36
consideration for others, 115–116
contemplation, 46, 173
    of the body, 52–57
    of consciousness, 109–110
    of experience, 149–184
    of feeling, 75–104
    of "I," xvi–xvii, 125–127
    of knowing, 105–148
    of mental states, 152–158
    of somatic activity, 51–74, 63*f*, 91
continuity field, 136–140
controlled processing, 37, 171
councils, 7–12, 14, 14*f*
creative activity, 122

D

Damasio, Antonio, 172
dark night, 147
Darmagupta school, 9
decentering, xv
declarative memory, 143–144
deconditioning, 88
deep vision, *see* Vipassana meditation
denomination, 122
desire, 86–90, 162*f*, 163
Dhamma, xxii
Dhammapada, 20
Dhammapala, 7, 14*f*
dhammas (mental phenomena), 42–43, 78, 95–97, 110–111, 125, 158
Dhiravamsa, 15
differential threshold, 73
Digha Nikaya, 20–21
dignity, 115–116
Dipa Ma, 14*f*

Discourse on the Four Foundations of Mindfulness, see Satipatthāna Sutta
dispersion of matter, 62–63, 63f, 73
dissatisfaction *(dukkha)*, 12, 25f, 45, 62, 88, 177
doubt, 153, 162, 162f
dry insight, 174
dukkha (dissatisfaction), 12, 25f, 45, 62, 88, 177

E
early Buddhism, 19–21
Eastern Buddhism, 6
ecstasy, 147
elements, 63f, 71–72
embodiment, 69
emotion(s), 131
    emotional intelligence, 94
    primary emotions, 140–141
    secondary emotions, 141
Emotional Intelligence (Goleman), 15
Emotional Quotient (EQ), 15
empty awareness, 180
enlightenment, 155–157
Enlightenment, xx
epigenetics, 83, 142
episodic memory, 143–144
equanimity, 103–104
ethics, xxii, 58, 172, *see also sila* (moral conduct)
eudaimonic values, 135–136
evaluative conditioning, 99
executive functions, 35f, 166
experience, 152
    contemplation of the phenomena of, 149–184
    first-person, xxi, 27, 29–31, 47, 160
    flow of, 158–160
    phenomena of, 125
    somatic, 66–67
    third-person, 29
experiential self, 137
external sense bases, 154–155

F
feeling(s), 46, 51, 76–79, 101–102
    immeasurable affective states, 103–104
    mental, 101
    vs. sensation, 39–42
    spiritual emotions, 103
feeling activity(-ies), 40, 76, 107
    as cognitive, 79–80
    contemplation of, 75–104
    innate vs acquired, 84–86
    intentions in action, xxi, 97
    intentions of action, xxi, 97
Feldenkrais Method, 69
first-person experience, xxi, 29, 160
    first-person knowledge of, 30–31, 47
    third-person knowledge of, 27, 29, 47
Five Aggregates of clinging, 150, 151f, 154
Five Hindrances, 152–154, 160–175, 162f
fixed concentration *(appana samadhi)*, 17
flow of experience, 158–160
forgetting, 169
formal practice, 70
Four Noble Truths, 18, 21–25, 25f, 150, 157–158
Four Postures, 54
free mind, 146–148
Fronsdal, Gil, xxii

G

generative practices, 59
Goenka, 14
Goldstein, Joseph, 14*f*
Goleman, Daniel, 14, 14*f*, 15
Gravobac, Andrea, xxii–xxiii
Greece, 5–6

H

habit, 82–84, 89*f*
healthy cognitive activity *(citta)*, 115–116, 115*f*, 123
heart, 127–128
The Heart of Buddhist Meditation (Nyanaponika Thera), 14
hedonic values, 135–136
hindrances, 152–154, 160–175, 162*f*
    affective, 163–166, 168, 170–172
    cognitive, 164–165, 168, 170–172
    liberation from, 171–175
    staying connected with *sati*, 166–168
    working with, 168–170
Hinduism, 4–5
history, 11
homeostasis, 128

I

"I"
    construction of, 80–82
    contemplating the concept of, xvi–xvii, 125–127
    illusion of, 180–181, 181*f*
    vs. "narrative I," 105, 137
    "proto-I," 80–82, 178
    transcendence of, 150–152
idealism, xvii
identity, 142–143
ill will, 162*f*, 163
immeasurable states of mind, 103–104
impermanence, 12, 25*f*, 45, 62, 177
impersonality, 62
India, 5, 10, 12
individual maturation, 150–152
informal practice, 70
inheritance, transgenerational, 83
innate reactions, 84–86, 88–89
Insight Meditation Society, 14*f*
insights, xxii–xxiii, 169
    dry, 174
    sixteen of Vipassana, 60, 61*f*, 101
    wet, 174
instinct, 82–84
Integral Vipassana, xvii–xx, 24, 25*f*
intellect *(manas)*, 135
intellect *(mano)*, 111
intention, 32, 145–146
    in action, xxi, 97
    of action, xxi, 97
    cetana, 135
internal sense bases, 154–155
interoception, 63*f*, 69–70
Iran, 9
Islam, 5–6
Israel, 5

J

Jainism, 4–6
Japan, 9, 12
Jatakas, 20
Jha, Amishi, xxii
jhanas, 13, 16–18, 60, 61*f*, 101, 148, 173
Judaism, 5–6

K

Kabat-Zinn, Jon, 15
Kahneman, Daniel, 30
Kalamas, 23
Kalama Sutta, 23
Kamalashila, 60, 60*f*
kamma (past action), 20
Kashmir, 9–10
Kesaputta, 23
khana paccuppanna (momentary present), 134
khanika samadhi (momentary concentration), 17
kinaesthesia, 74
knowing, 107–109, *see also* insights
    activities of, 107
    bhavanga, 129
    citta (cognitive activity), 106–119, 115*f*, 123–125, 129–130, 135
    contemplation of the activities of knowing, 105–148
    first knowledge of Vipassana, 52
    first-person knowledge of first-person experience, 30–31, 47
    human knowledge, xvi
    sixteen levels of Vipassana knowledge, 60, 61*f*, 101
    third-person knowledge of first-person experience, 27, 29, 47
Korea, 9
Kornfield, Jack, 14, 14*f*
Kushán dynasty, 10
Kuthodaw Pagoda, 10, 14*f*

L

language, 131
Laos, 12
lapsus, 169

latent tendencies, 179
learned behavior, 82, 97
learning, 131
learning by consequences, 99
lethargy, 162*f*, 163
liberation from hindrances, 171–175
Loy, David, xv–xvi

M

Magadha, 11
Maha Bodhi Society, 7, 14*f*
Mahaparinibbana, 20
Maharashtri, 6
Mahasanghika school, 21
Mahasatipattana Sutta, 21
Mahasi Sayadaw, 11–12, 14, 14*f*
Mahayana Buddhism, 8, 22
Mahīsāsaka school, 22
Majjhima Nikaya, 20–21
manas (intellect), 135
Mandalay, Burma, 10
mano (intellect), 111
manoviññana (mind consciousness), 111
mantras, 26
material elements, reflection on, 55
materialism, xvii
materiality, subtle, 83, 87, 112, 117
material phenomena, 95–97
matter *(rupa)*, 67–68, 124–125, 158, 181*f*
    dispersion of, 62–63, 63*f*, 73
    mind and matter *(namarupa)*, 69, 74, 108, 118–119, 177
maturation, xviii, xviii*f*, 150–152
Maurya kingdom, 6
McMindfulness, xvi
meditation, 57–62
    compassion, 26

Index

concentration, *see* Samatha meditation
conscious attention, *see* sati
contemplation of experience, 149–184
contemplation of feeling, 75–104
contemplation of "I," xvi–xvii, 125–127
contemplation of knowing, 105–148
contemplation of mental states, 152–158
contemplation of somatic activity, 51–74, 63f, 91
deep vision, *see* Vipassana meditation
focused attention, *see* samadhi
generative practices, 59
liberation from hindrances, 171–175
in motion, 69
New Burmese Method, 12
sixteen insights of, xxii–xxiii, 60, 61f, 101
Thai, 15
types of practice, xviii, xviiif
visualization during, 125
work with the Five Aggregates of clinging, 150, 151f
meditation objects, 58–59
memory, 130, 140–146
    declarative, 143–144
    episodic, 143–144
    long-term, 131
    non-declarative, 143–144
    of oneself, 131–140
    procedural, 143
    semantic, 143–145
    sensory, 132

    short-term, 131
    working, 132–134, 136–140
mental consciousness *(viññana)*, 111, 135
mental factors *(cetasikas)*, 83, 108, 114–116, 116f, 124–125, 130, 135
mental feeling, 101
mentalization, xv
mental perception, xv
mental phenomena *(dhammas)*, 42–43, 78, 95–97, 110–111, 125, 158
mental processes, 113–116
    attention networks, xx–xxi, 25f, 34f, 35f, 36, 41–42
    automatic, 37–38, 171
    basic factors *(cetasikas)*, 83, 108, 114–116, 116f, 131
    "bottom-up," 25, 30, 41–42, 117
    complex, 131
    conscious, 36
    controlled, 37, 171
    healthy, 115–116, 115f
    integration with spiritual awakening, 25, 25f
    parallel processing, 112
    "top-down" processes, 25, 30, 41–42, 87, 117, 170
    unconscious processing, 36, 113
mental stability, *see* samadhi
mental states, 103–104, 152–158
mental training *(bhavana)*, 59, 114, 127
meta-attentional practices, 59
metacognition, xv
metaconsciousness, xix, 69, 139
mind *(nama)*, 69–70, 158, 181f
mind and matter *(namarupa)*, 69, 74, 108, 118–119, 177
mind-body connection, 90–97
mind consciousness *(manoviññana)*, 111

mindfulness, xiv–xv, 15, 24, 99, 130–140, 173–174
   of breathing, 52–53
   with clear comprehension, 54
   as cognitive activity, 122–124
   formal practice of, 70
   foundations of, 25, 25f, 31–32, 44–45
   informal practice of, 70
   McMindfulness, xvi
   mechanisms of, xxii–xxiii
   modern, 175–176
Mindón, 10
mind wandering, 138–139
Mingun Sayadaw (U Nārada), 12–14, 14f
momentary concentration (*khanika samadhi*), 17
momentary configurations, 133
momentary present (*khana paccuppanna*), 134
monastic rules (*Vinaya Pitaka*), 8–9, 19
Mongolia, 10
monotheism, 5
motion, meditation in, 69
motivation(s), 97, 131
Mulasarvastivada school, 10
Munindra, 14, 14f
Myanmar, 10

N

nama (mind), 69–70, 158, 181f
nama-paññatti (name-concept), 134
namarupa (mind and matter), 69, 74, 108, 118–119, 177
"narrative I," 105
narrative self, 137
Nepal, 12

neurophenomenology, xxi
neuropsychoanalysis, xxi
neuroscience, xxi, xxii
New Burmese Method, 12
nibbana (awakening), 16, 124, 181f
nine cemetery contemplations, 55–57
Noble Eightfold Path, 18, 21–25, 25f, 57–58, 150
non-attachment, 115–116, 124
non-attentive activity, 170–171
non-aversion, 115–116
non-self (*anatta*), 12, 25f, 45, 126, 177
"now," 133–134
nuclear self, 81, 178
Nyanaponika Thera, 12, 14, 14f, 75
Nyanasatta Thera, 31–32
Nyanatiloka, 12

O

observer trap, 176
obstacles, 67
oneself, *see* self
operant conditioning, 99
"other," xvi–xvii, 115–116, 150–152

P

paccuppanna (present), 134
pain, 167
Pakistan, 9–10
Pali, 6–7
Pali Canon (*Tipitaka*), 9–11, 14f
   additional teachings (*Abhidhamma Pitaka*), 9–10, 19–21, 106–108, 139
   Discourse on the Four Foundations of Mindfulness (Satipatthāna Sutta), *see* Satipatthāna Sutta
   Edition of the Sixth Council, 10, 12

Index

monastic rules *(Vinaya Pitaka),* 8–9, 19
speeches, *see Sutta Pitaka*
Pali Text Society, 7
Panksepp, Jaak, xxi
paññā (intention), 18, 25, 25*f*, 34, 57–58
paññati (apparent, conventional, or compound reality), 113, 124
parallel processing, 112
paramattha (ulimate or irreducible reality), 124–125
Parayana Sutta, 51
Paticca-samuppada causality (dependent origination), 12
perception, 38, 92, 107, 134
    intention and, 145–146
    memory and, 143–146
    in psychology, 131
Persia, 5
perspicacity, xix
phenomena
    composite, 124–125
    contemplation of the phenomena of experience, 149–184
    of experience, 125
    material, 95–97
    mental *(dhammas),* 42–43, 78, 95–97, 110–111, 125, 158
    neurophenomenology, xxi
philosophy, 5
physiological activities, 63*f*, 70–71
Pitaka Sutta, 19–20, 34
    Anguttara Nikaya, v, 20, 105
    Digha Nikaya, 20–21
    Khuddaka-Nikaya, 20
    Majjhima Nikaya, 20–21
    Samyutta Nikaya, 20–21
Posner, Michael, xx–xxi

Prajnaparamita Sutras, 22, 90
Prakrit, 6
pre-consciousness, 44
preliminary concentration *(upacara samadhi),* 17
present *(paccuppanna),* 134
present in series *(santati paccuppanna),* 135–136
primary emotions, 140–141
priming, 99
procedural memory, 143
proprioception, 63*f*, 68–69, 118
"proto-I," 80–82, 178
Pudgalavada school, 22

R

rational activity, 120
reaction, 86–90
reality
    apparent, conventional, or compound *(paññati),* 113, 124
    conditioned realities *(sankharas),* 112, 124–125
    vs. continuity field, 136–140
    ult
    imate realities *(paramatthas),* 124–125
recitation of mantras, 26
rediscoveries, 169
referential frameworks, 122
reflexes, 97–101
remorse, 153
reperception, xv
representations, 112–113
restlessness, 162*f*, 163
Rhys Davids, T.W., 7
Royal Library of Denmark, 7
rupa (matter), 67–68, 124–125, 158, 181*f*

dispersion of, 62–63, 63f, 73
namarupa (mind and matter), 69, 74, 108, 118–119, 177
Russia, 10

S

Sabba Sutta, 149
Salzberg, Sharon, 14f
samadhi (focused attention), xxi, 16–18, 22–25, 25f, 33–34, 35f, 43, 57–60, 174
    appana samadhi, 17
    development of, 60, 60f
    elements of, 184
    hindrances to, 152–154, 160–175, 162f
    khanika samadhi, 17
    vs. sati, 131–132, 137
    upacara samadhi, 17
Samatha meditation, xviii, xviiif, 22–23, 59, 136–137, 174
    history of, 15–18
    yanika, 67
sampajañña, 69–70
Sampasadaniya, 20
Samyutta Nikaya, 20–21, 51
Sanghadeva, 21
sankharas (conditioned realities), 112, 124–125
Sanskrit, 6, 10
santati paccuppanna ("present in series"), 135–136
S-ART framework, xxii
Sarvāstivāda school, 9–10, 21–22
sati (conscious attention), 17–18, 22–27, 25f, 33–36, 35f, 43, 46–47, 59–60, 183–184
    as cognitive activity, 122–124
    development of, 60, 61f, 173–174
    as meditation, 12, 15–16
    as memory, 131–132, 137–143
    non-attentive activity and, 170–171
    vs. samadhi, 131–132, 137
    staying connected, 166–168
    and transcendence, 175–178
    working with hindrances, 168–170
Satipatthāna, xiv, 36, 59, 70
Satipatthāna (term), 21
Satipatthāna Sutta (Discourse on the Four Foundations of Mindfulness), 3, 12, 16, 19–23, 30
    Chinese versions, 21, 90
    conclusion, 183
    on contemplation of consciousness, 109–110
    on contemplation of feeling, 77–78
    on contemplation of mental states, 152–158
    on contemplation of the body, 52–58
    first three paragraphs, 31–32, 34–41, 44
    Pali version, 21, 90
    refrain, 45–47
    translations, 31–32, 90
Sayadaw (term), 11
scientific method, 92
scripture(s), 5–7, 14
secondary emotions, 141
self
    autobiographical, 178
    experiential, 137
    "I," xvi–xvii, 80–82, 180–181, 181f
    memory of oneself, 131–140
    narrative, 137
    "narrative I," 105

nuclear, 81, 178
"proto-I," 80–82, 178
self-regulation systems, 25f
self-transcendence, xxii, 129–130
semantic memory, 143–145
sensation(s), 51–52, 73, 78–79
    carnal, 92
    vs. feeling, 39–42
    six internal and external sense bases, 154–155
    spiritual, 92, 101–102
sense spheres, 176
sensory memory, 132
sensuous desire, 162f, 163
serenity, 137, 147, 179
set, 57
setting, 57
seven factors of enlightenment, 155–157
sexual desire, 162f, 163
Sikhism, 6
sila (moral conduct), 18, 25, 25f, 34, 57–58, 145
Silk Road, 10
Sinhalese monks, 9
six internal and external sense bases, 154–155
sixteen insights of Vipassana, xxii–xxiii, 60, 61f, 101
Sixth Buddhist Council, 10–12, 14f
sloth and torpor, 153, 162f, 163
Sobin, 15
soma, 4
somatic activity(-ies), 40, 107
    contemplation of, 51–74, 91
    how to observe, 62–63, 63f
somatic experience, 66–67, 69
somatic markers, 172
Southern India, 9
space, 118–119
speeches, see *Sutta Pitaka*
    Discourse on the Four Foundations of Mindfulness (*Satipatthāna Sutta*), see *Satipatthāna Sutta*
spiritual awakening, xviiif, 150–152
spiritual emotions, 103
spirituality, 13
Spiritual Quotient (SQ), 15
spiritual sensations, 92, 101–102
Sri Lanka, 9, 12
Sthaviras, 21–22
subtle materiality, 83, 87, 112, 117
Sutta Pitaka (speeches), 8–9, 19–20, 34
    Anapanasati Sutta, 64
    Kalama Sutta, 23
    Mahasatipattana Sutta, 21
    Parayana Sutta, 51
    Sabba Sutta, 149
    Satipatthāna Sutta, see *Satipatthāna Sutta*
    Sutta-Nipata, 20

T

Tai Chi, 69
Tajikistan, 10
Taoism, 5–6
temperature, 124
ten stages of *Kamalashila*, 60, 60f
Thailand, 12
Thai meditation, 15
thana (desire), 86
theory of mind, xv, 141
Theravada Buddhism, xxiii
    councils, 9–12, 14, 14f
    history, 8–10
    mental factors, 116, 116f
    primary emotions, 141

scriptures, 6–7, 14f
Theravada school, 21–22
"thing concept" (atthapaññatti), 134
third-person experience, 29
third-person knowledge of first-person experience, 27, 29, 47
thought, 131
thought drifts, 138–139
three poisons, 141–143
Tibetan Buddhism, 10, 14–15
time, 118–119
time travel, 178
Tipitaka, see Pali Canon
"top-down" processes, 25, 30, 41–42, 87, 117, 170
transcendence, 174–178
transgenerational inheritance, 83
trust, 115–116
truth, 180–182

U

Udaka Ramaputta, 64
Udana, 20
ulimate reality (paramattha dhamma), 124–125
U Ñanadhaja, 14f
U Nārada (Mingun Sayadaw), 12–14, 14f
unconscious processing, 36, 113
upacara samadhi (preliminary concentration), 17
upadana (attachment), 86
U Pandita, 14, 14f, 15
Upanishads, 4
Uzbekistan, 10

V

Vago, Dave, xxii
values and virtues, 135–136
Varela, Francisco J., xxi
vayama, xxi, 16–18, 22–25, 25f, 34, 35f, 60, 164–165

Vedas, 4
Vedism, 4–5
verbal activity, 120
Vibhajyavāda school, 22
Vietnam, 9, 12
Vinaya Pitaka (monastic rules), 8–9, 19
viññana (mental consciousness), 111, 135
Vipassana meditation, xiv–xx, xviiif, 27, 43–45, 59, 175, 184
  history of, 11–18
  New Burmese Method, 12
  objective of, 176
  sixteen insights of, xxii–xxiii, 60, 61f, 101, 174
  work with the Five Aggregates of clinging, 150, 151f
  yanika, 67
Vipassana movement, 11–16, 14f
vipassanavada, 16
vision
  deep vision meditation, 13
  wrong, 142
visual awareness (cakkuviññana), 111, 159
visualization, 125
Visuddhimagga, 7, 14f
vital faculty, 83, 87, 146

W

Western thinking, 90
wet insight, 174
Wilber, Ken, xvii–xviii, xix, xx, 23
wisdom, 25, 27
working memory, 132–134, 136–140
wrong views, 151f
wrong vision, 142

Y

Yoga, 69

Z

Zen Buddhism, 14–15
Zoroastrianism, 5

www.ingramcontent.com/pod-product-compliance
Lightning Source LLC
Chambersburg PA
CBHW060513100426
42743CB00009B/1300